HELP

TO

ZION'S TRAVELLERS:

BEING AN

ATTEMPT TO REMOVE VARIOUS STUMBLING
BLOCKS OUT OF THE WAY,

RELATING TO

DOCTRINAL, EXPERIMENTAL AND
PRACTICAL RELIGION.

BY REV. ROBERT HALL, OF ARNSBY.

Philadelphia:
AMERICAN BAPTIST PUBLICATION SOCIETY,
118 ARCH STREET

PHILADELPHIA:
STEREOTYPED BY GEORGE CHARLES.

ADVERTISEMENT.

THE Publication Society here presents the christian public with a most important work. Its republication will, it is hoped, avail much in keeping up old landmarks and removing the obscurity which embarrasses so many, in relation to cardinal doctrines.

No work on practical piety is superior to Hall's Help, as a brief, intelligible, devout, and scriptural elucidation of the topics on which it treats.

The book has been carefully edited by Rev. Howard Malcom, D. D., at the request of the Society. A comparison with old editions will at once show the extent of the changes, which consist chiefly in modernizing the style in some places, correcting numerous errors in the references, and arranging chapters, paragraphs, quotations, &c. No sentiment is added or omitted, or any change made in the general style of the author. Some notes from a former edition, by Rev. Jos. A. Warne, are inserted, and marked with his initials.

CONTENTS.

PART I.

DOCTRINAL DIFFICULTIES.

CHAPTER I.

CHAPTER II.

CHAPTER III.

CHAPTER IV.

CHAPTER V.

CHAPTER VI.

PART II.

EXPERIMENTAL DIFFICULTIES.

CHAPTER I.

CHAPTER II.

CHAPTER III.

CHAPTER IV.

CHAPTER V.

CHAPTER VI.

PART III.

PRACTICAL DIFFICULTIES.

CHAPTER I.

CHAPTER II

CHAPTER III.

PREFACE

TO THE

SECOND LONDON EDITION.

BY REV. DR. RYLAND.

TWENTY-EIGHT years have elapsed since that Sermon was delivered, in my father's pulpit, at Northampton, before the Baptist Association, which Mr. *Hall* afterwards enlarged into the following Treatise. As I then united with many others in earnestly soliciting its publication, so I have since repeatedly perused it with much satisfaction. When, therefore, the publisher of the present edition applied to me for a recommendatory preface, I felt no hesitation but what arose from the early impressions of veneration for one of the wisest and best of men, to whom I was habituated to look up with such respect, as made this office feel to me assuming and arrogant. But when I reflect that he has been removed from our world for more than sixteen years, (and verily I miss no man more!) and consider that, since his decease, many have joined our churches, who never had opportunity duly to appreciate his worth; it seems not to be taking too much upon me, to testify in what high estimation he was justly held by those who had the pleasure of his acquaintance. Strong natural powers, ardent piety, deep exercises of mind, a series of singular and sanctified trials, with a special unction from the Holy One, rendered him a man of quick understanding in the fear of the Lord.

Deeply convinced of human guilt and depravity, and very zealous for the honor of sovereign grace; but no less concerned for internal holiness and practical religion; he was careful to walk in the midst of the paths of judgment, and to beware of turning aside to the right hand or the left.

He called no man upon earth master, in respect of his religious sentiments, but he took a peculiar delight in the writings of President EDWARDS; and two Sermons by Mr. *Smalley,* (which I borrowed of our venerable friend Mr. *Newton,* of *Olney,* and after transcribing them, lent them to Mr. *Hall,*) contributed much to strengthen his conviction, that the *moral impotence* of sinners is no more an excuse for their slighting the *call of the gospel,* than it is for their violating the *commands of the law.* As the greatest disinclination to regard Divine *authority* cannot release a rational creature from an obligation to obey God's *precepts;* so the utter aversion of a sinner to regard the *kindness* of God our Saviour, cannot release him from an obligation thankfully to comply with his *invitations.*

At the same time, Mr. *Hall* remained as strenuous an advocate as ever for the necessity and efficacy of divine influence, to induce sinners or saints to comply cordially with their indispensable duty; and he was more abundantly confirmed in a belief of the sovereign freeness of grace, by reflecting that the inexcusable perverseness of the human heart, which renders the agency of the divine Spirit so necessary, must at the same time evince that we are utterly unworthy of his gracious interposition. The greater our reluctance is to come unto God, in the way which he has prescribed for our return, the more undeserving are we of being drawn unto him by his Holy Spirit.

But this excellent man remarked, that if the invitations of the gospel are *not indefinite*, or addressed to *sinners* considered simply as *needy* and *guilty*, there can be no foundation for the *first* act of faith; the sinner can have no warrant for his application to Christ, unless he could know his election, or prove his regeneration, before he committed his soul to him. Hence, as he once observed in a letter to a friend, they who would restrict the call of the gospel, "ought in reason to point out how unbelievers may know their election or regeneration in order to warrant their *first* application to Christ; or how the assurance of personal interest in Christ may be obtained, *before* persons *come* to him. The first acts of faith must be unwarrantable and presumptuous, if there be no previous call or invitation. We allow a change of heart must precede faith, but *unknown renovation* cannot be the ground of the sinner's first encouragement to apply to the Saviour; or that on which his right to confide in him is founded, because it is unknown. And to suppose any *knowledge* of regeneration or a change of heart, *in order to* a reliance on Jesus, is the same as supposing an assurance of possessing the spirit and grace of God, while an unbeliever; or that a man must *know* he is really safe, before he *flees* from danger."

This little volume, however, is far from being confined to a subject on which Mr. Hall, in his latter years, thought differently from the opinion he had embraced at his first setting out in the ministry. It contains an able vindication of the genuine doctrines of grace, from the objections of Socinians, Sabellians, Arminians, and Antinomians. At its first publication, it was much approved by many pious, judicious, and learned men, of different denominations; and here that excellent man, who is now laboring in India, with such indefatigable zeal for the salvation of the heathen, first found his own system of divinity. Raised from the greatest obscurity, Mr. *Carey* had but little access to books, at his first setting out in religion; and perplexed between the statements of the *Arminians,* and the crude representations of Calvinism, by persons bordering closely on *Antinomianism,* he searched the Scriptures attentively for himself, endeavoring to find out the narrow way, between extremes which seemed irreconcilable to the honor of divine *government,* and the glory of divine *grace*: and this was the first summary of evangelical truth, which appeared to him fully to accord with the sacred standard.

On one particular which many readers might expect Mr. *Hall* to have noticed, he has hardly touched, viz. *the denial of the law of God as a rule of conduct to believers.* This sentiment he *ever* considered as so gross a piece of *Antinomianism,* that he did not suppose any man could embrace it, whose conscience was not seared as with a hot iron. The eminent divines, who verged to an extreme respecting the obligation of sinners to repent and believe the gospel, would have reprobated *this* doctrine, as tending to the greatest licentiousness. Dr. *Gill*, Mr. *Brine*, Mr. *Toplady*, &c., utterly condemned so vile a sentiment. But within the last twenty years how many who exclaimed against Mr. *Hall* and his brethren, for embracing *new* sentiments respecting the *duty of sinners*, have readily departed from their former guides, and embraced *new* notions respecting the *duty of believers!*

To me it appears a most marvellous instance of the deceitfulness of sin, if any man can think himself a friend to evangelical religion, who by sinking *unbelievers below* all obligation, and raising *believers above* all obligation, almost annihilates both duty and sin, and so leaves no room for the exercise of either pardoning mercy or sanctifying grace. The apostolic axiom, "where there is no law there is no transgression," justly leads us to conclude, that they who are below or above law have no guilt, and need no Saviour; there is no room to show the riches of his grace, or the efficacy of his blood, in the pardon of those who never deserved punishment. If the commmand be exceedingly narrow, our sins must be very few, and the pardon of them a small matter. And if the *effectual influence* of the Spirit be supposed to be the source, rule, and measure of Obligation, no one can have reason to mourn for sin; since he always does as much as he was powerfully inclined to do, and by this supposition it was not his duty to do any more. Thus sinless perfection is easily attained, though in the backward way; not by coming up to the standard of rectitude, but by bringing it down to our level. Most comfortable doctrine to a carnal heart!

May God bless the reprinting of this excellent work, to lead many more fully into the truth as it is in Christ Jesus, is the earnest prayer of

The reader's cordial friend,

And servant, for Christ's sake,

JOHN RYLAND.

PREFACE

TO THE

THIRD LONDON EDITION.

BY REV. ROBERT HALL, Jr., A. M.

An aversion to religious controversy may arise from two causes, in their nature the most opposite; a contempt of religion itself, or a high degree of devotional feeling. They who consider the objects of religion as visionary and uncertain, or who, rejecting revelation, feel their inability to find a place where they may fix their footing, will naturally feel an emotion of contempt for theological contests, similar to that which we should experience towards men who were fighting for possessions in the air.

There are not a few who would engage with the utmost seriousness and ardor in a dispute on the nature and effects of paper currency, who would be ashamed of being suspected of directing their attention for a moment to the most weighty questions in theology. Attentive to all the aspects and combinations of the material and of the political world, they are accustomed to regard religion as a sort of Utopia, a land of shadow and of fiction, where, wrapt in pleasing vision, Credulity reposes on the lap of Imposture. This sort of persons are so completely overcome by the enchantments of the present state, so entirely devoted to the wisdom which St. James denominates earthly and sensual, that they are incapable of being impressed with a conviction of the possibility of a higher order of objects, or a more elevated and refined condition of being, than that with which they are conversant; and though they may possess a subtle and penetrating genius, they are not less disqualified for religious inquiries than an idiot or an infant. *They mind earthly things.*

How far the indisposition to religious controversy which prevails at present, may be justly ascribed to this Sadducean temper, I shall not pretend to determine. It is certain, however, that, in some, this indisposition proceeds from a better cause. While the former class of persons think religion not worth disputing about, there are others who conceive it to be a subject too sacred for dispute. They wish to confine it to silent meditation, to sweeten solitude, to inspire devotion, to guide the practice, and purify the heart, and never to appear in public but in the character of the authentic interpreter of the will of Heaven. They conceive it degraded whenever it is brought forward to combat on the arena. We are fully convinced, that a disputatious humor is unfavorable to piety; and that controversies in religion have often been unnecessarily multiplied and extended; but how they can be dispensed with altogether, we are at a loss to discover, until some other method is discovered of confuting error, than sound and solid argument. As we no longer live in times (God be thanked!) when coercion can be employed, or when any individual, or any body of men, are invested with that authority which could silence disputes by an oracular decision, there appears no possibility of maintaining the interests of truth, without having recourse to temperate and candid controversy. Perhaps the sober use of this weapon may not be without its advantages, even at the present season. Prone as we are to extremes, may there not be some reason to apprehend, we have passed from that propensity to magnify every difference subsisting among Christians, to a neglect of just discrimination, to a habit of contemplating the christian system as one in which there is little or nothing that remains to be explored. Let us cultivate the most cordial esteem for all that love the Lord Jesus Christ in sincerity. Let us anxiously guard against that asperity and contempt which have too often mingled with theological debates; but let us aim, at the same time, to acquire and retain the most accurate conceptions of religious truth. Every improvement in the knowledge of Christ and the mysteries of his Gospel, will abundantly compensate for the labor and attention necessary to its attainment.

However unhappily controversies have too often been conducted, the assistance they have afforded in the discovery of truth, is not light nor inconsiderable. Not to mention the Reformation, which was principally effected by controversy, how many truths have, by this means, been set in a clearer view; and when the unhappy passions it has awakened have subsided, the light struck out in the collision has been retained and perpetuated.

As the physical powers are scarcely ever exerted to their utmost extent, but in the ardor of combat, so intellectual acumen has been displayed to the most advantage, and to the most effect, in the contests of argument. The mind of a controversialist, warmed and agitated, is turned to all quarters, and leaves none of its resources unemployed in the invention of arguments, tries every weapon, and explores the hidden recesses of a subject with an intense vigilance and an ardor which it is next to impossible, in a calmer state of mind, to command. Disingenuous arts are often resorted to, personalities are mingled, and much irritative matter is introduced; but it is the business of the attentive observer to separate these from the question at issue, and to form an impartial judgment of the whole. In a word, it may be truly affirmed that the evils occasioned by controversy are transient; the good it produces is permanent.

The sentiments of my honored father were decidedly Calvinistic. His object, however, in the following treatise, was not so much to recommend that system in general, as to disengage it from certain excrescences, which he considered as weakening its evidence and impairing its beauty. On reviewing his religious tenets during the latter years of his life, and impartially comparing them with the Scriptures, he was led to discard some opinions which he had formerly embraced, and which he afterwards came to consider as having a pernicious tendency.

From the moral impotence which the oracles of truth ascribe to man in his fallen state, a certain class of divines were induced to divide moral and religious duties into two classes, natural and spiritual; comprehending under the latter, those which require spiritual or supernatural assistance to their performance; and under the former, those which demand no such assistance. Agreeable to this distinction, they conceived it to be the duty of all men to abstain from the outward acts of sin, to read the Scriptures, to frequent the worship of God, and to attend with serious assiduity to the means of grace; but they supposed that repentance, faith in Christ, and the exercise of genuine internal devotion, were obligatory only on the regenerate. Hence their ministry consisted almost entirely of an exhibition of the peculiar mysteries of the gospel, with few or no addresses to the unconverted. They conceived themselves not warranted to urge them to repent and believe the gospel, those being spiritual duties, from whose obligation they were released by the inability contracted by the fall.

These conclusions were evidently founded upon two assumptions; first, that the impotence which the Scriptures ascribe to the unregenerate is free from blame, so as to excuse them from all the duties to which it extends. In opposition to this, the author of the following treatise has proved, in a very satisfactory manner, that the inability under which the unconverted labor, is altogether of a moral nature, consisting in the corruption of the will, or an aversion to things of a spiritual and divine nature; that it is in itself criminal; and that, so far from affording an excuse for what would otherwise be duty, it stamps with its own character all its issues and productions.

In considering the moral character of an action, we are naturally led to inquire into its motive, and according as that is criminal, laudable or indifferent, to characterize the action whence it proceeds. The motive, however, appears no otherwise entitled to commendation, than as it indicates the disposition of the agent; so that in analyzing the elements of moral character, we can ascend no higher than to the consideration of the disposition, or the state of the will and of the affections, as constituting the essence of that portion of virtue or of vice which we respectively ascribe to it. To proceed farther will only involve us in a circle, since to whatever we might trace the disposition in question, should we be induced, for example, to ascribe it to the free exercise of the will, that exercise would fall under the same predicament, and be considered either as virtuous or vicious, according to the disposition whence it proceeds. When the Scriptures have placed the inability of mankind to yield holy and acceptable obedience in an evil disposition, or in blindness and hardness of heart, they have conducted us to the ultimate point on this subject, and have established the doctrine of human criminality upon a basis which cannot be shaken or disturbed, without confounding the first principles of moral discrimination. Though it is manifest this impotence is entirely of a moral nature, totally distinct from the want of natural faculties, it is equally evident, that to whatever extent it exists, while it actually subsists, it is as effectual an impediment to the performance of holy actions as any physical privation whatever; and on that account, and that alone, may, without absurdity, be styled an *inability*.* This important dis-

*This truth is lost sight of by those preachers among us, who assert "that it is as easy to give up the affec-

tinction was not altogether unknown to our earlier divines, though they neglected to avail themselves of it as fully as they ought. It is clearly stated by the great Mr. Howe, in his Blessedness of the Righteous, as well as adverted to by Mr. Baxter in several of his practical works. But the earliest regular treatise on this subject it has been my lot to meet with, was the production of Mr. Towman, an eminent non-conformist divine. In his dissertation on moral impotence, as he styles it, he has anticipated the most important arguments of succeeding writers, and has evinced, throughout, a most masterly acquaintance with his subject.

Another principle assumed as a basis by the high Calvinists, is, that the same things cannot be the duty of man, and the gift of God: or, in other words, that what is matter of promise, can on no occasion, be the matter of obligation. The Scriptures frequently affirm faith and repentance to be the gifts of God; hence it is concluded that they cannot be obligatory on the unregenerate; a conclusion diametrically opposed to innumerable passages in the Old and New Testament, which insist, in the most peremptory style, on true conversion and a lively faith, as the most essential duties, which other passages are equally express in exhibiting as matter of promise. *A new heart will I give them*, says the Lord by Ezekiel, *and a new spirit will I put within them, and I will take away the heart of stone, and give them a heart*

tions to God as it is to rise from our seat." The difference in *nature* between physical and moral inability, does not destroy the *reality* of either: the latter is as *real* as the former, and may be as absolute. J. A. W.

of flesh. The same prophet cries, *Make you a new heart, for why will ye die, O house of Israel?* in exact accordance with the language of St. James, *Cleanse your hands, ye sinners, and purify your hearts, ye double-minded.* The burden of our Saviour's ministry, as well as that of his forerunner, was, *Repent, for the kingdom of God is at hand;* while St. Peter, who perfectly knew the genius of Christianity, affirms that Christ is *exalted to give repentance and the remission of sins. Circumcise your hearts,* said Moses, *and be no longer stiff-necked:* the same Moses had been previously commissioned to declare, *The Lord thy God shall circumcise thine heart and the heart of thy seed.* Now the circumcision of the heart we are taught by St. Paul in his Epistle to the Romans, to regard as the distinguishing feature of the truly regenerate—*of him who is a Jew inwardly, whose praise is not of man, but of God.* Whoever impartially weighs the import of these Scriptures, must be convinced that the same things are, in *fact,* matter of command, and the subject of promise, and must, consequently, be prepared to acquiesce in the decision of infinite wisdom on this subject, however much he may be at a loss to explain or account for it. The consistency of the promises and of the commands in question, arises from the matter of each being of a moral nature. If we will allow ourselves to reflect, we shall perceive that the will, and the will only, is the proper object of command, and that an agent is no otherwise accountable, or susceptible of moral government, than as he is the subject of voluntary powers: we shall also perceive that the disordered state of the will, or the radical indisposition of an agent to comply with legitimate commands, which is the same thing, by no means exempts him from their obligation, nor tends in the least degree to render the addressing such commands to him absurd or improper. That they will not be complied with while that disordered state subsists, is true: but legitimate commands, enforced by proper sanctions, are amongst the strongest motives; that is, they tend in their own nature to incline the will, and therefore they cannot be withheld, without virtually relinquishing the claim of authority and dominion. This may suffice to evince the propriety of issuing commands, notwithstanding the known and radical indisposition to comply; or, which comes to the same thing, whatever be the *state of the will.* With respect to the other side of the supposed contradiction, what can be plainer than that the will, as well as every other faculty of the mind, is under divine control, and that God can with infinite ease, in what instances, and in what manner he please, so change and modify it, as to induce a prompt and cheerful compliance with his requisition? What should prevent him, at whose disposal are the hearts of the mightiest of men, *to make his people willing in the day of his power?*

It is instructive, as well as amusing, to trace the coincidence which is often found betwixt systems which appear at first view at the utmost variance from each other. The grosser Arminians and Pelagians contend, that it is the duty of all men to repent and believe, because all possess an inherent power of so doing, without special or supernatural assistance. The high Calvinists, on the contrary, deny that any man in a state of unregeneracy is under an obligation to perform those duties, because they are *not* possessed of the requisite ability. Thus both concur in making moral ability the measure of obligation; a position which, when the terms are accurately defined and cleared of their ambiguity, conducts us to this very extraordinary conclusion, that men are obliged to just as much of duty as they are inclined to. On these, and other points connected with them, the reader, if we are not mistaken, will find much solid instruction in the following Treatise, accompanied with such a constant attention to the great end of theological discussion, the promotion of practical piety, as can scarcely fail of affording high satisfaction to serious minds. To this Treatise, and to another on a similar subject, by my excellent and judicious friend, Mr. Fuller, the Dissenters in general, and the Baptists in particular, are under great obligations, for emancipating them from the fetters of prejudice, and giving free scope to the publication of the gospel. By these means a considerable revolution has been effected in the sentiments of the denomination to which I have the honor to belong: the excrescences of Calvinism have been cut off; the points of defence have been diminished in number, and better fortified; truth has shone forth with brighter lustre, and the ministry of the gospel has been rendered more simple, more practical, and more efficacious.

In reply to such as may object to the metaphysical subtlety which pervades some parts of the following Treatise, I would avail myself of the distinction admirably illustrated by Tucker, in his "Light of Nature pursued." He observes, that although metaphysical reasoning rarely, if ever, conduces to the discovery of truth, it is of great advantage in the detection of sophistry; and that the mist and confusion in which moral subjects have been involved, by crude and undigested metaphysics, can only be exploded by the temperate use of that which is true and genuine; so that the chief praise of metaphysics is the cure of its own ills, the repair of the mischief which itself has wrought. The reader will observe, that the author employs metaphysics, not to rear the fabric of truth, which can only be effected by a profound deference to inspiration, but to demolish a rotten superstition which conceals its beauty.

Gratitude and veneration compel me to add, that with all the imperfections of the work, and the disadvantages under which the author of it labored, I shall ever esteem it one of the greatest favors an indulgent Providence has conferred upon me, to have possessed such a father, whom in all the essential features of character it will be my humble ambition to imitate, though conscious it must ever be

—— Haud passibus æquis.

ROBERT HALL.

Sept. 1824.

PART I.

DOCTRINAL DIFFICULTIES.

CHAPTER I.

THE DEITY OF CHRIST.

It is only from the sacred Scriptures we can have information respecting the person and work of our precious Redeemer: to these he appealed in the days of his flesh, saying, Search the Scriptures, for they testify of me: but with what deceitfulness is the word of God handled by many, when the person of Christ is the subject of inquiry! Instances might easily be multiplied; but I shall mention only the following.

1. Some, in order to overthrow his claim to divinity, and the supreme love of his people, have collected passages of Scripture, which plainly declare his inferiority to God: from which they infer, with an appearance of good will to truth, that

as Scripture is evidently consistent with itself, he therefore who is therein declared to be inferior to deity, cannot possibly be divine. But a little attention is sufficient to discover that art is substituted in the room of argument, and sophistry occupies the place of sense. Every good man will rejoice in the harmony and consistency of divine revelation, and readily allow that inferiority and equality are opposites, and that in *the sense* in which Christ is spoken of as inferior, he is not, cannot be equal with God.

But as in the person of Christ two distinct natures are united, in consequence of which he is Immanuel, God with us; it does not follow, because he has a nature inferior to God, yea, even to angels, that his superior nature is not properly divine. Ten thousand testimonies in proof of his humanity do not in the least degree enervate his claim to deity: those who maintain the divinity of the blessed Saviour, as firmly believe him to be properly man, as they do who deny him to be God over all.

It is our unspeakable felicity, that the Son of God was sent into the world as a Mediator, to make peace between Jehovah in his public character as a governor, and rebellious men, that the Lord God might dwell among them, and they with him. In order to accomplish which, it was necessary he should assume human nature, and dwell among us. To reconcile God and man, it was needful he should be *a middle person, possessing the nature of both*, and as equally interested in favor of each party, be able to establish Heaven's righteous claim, and raise self-ruined man to a state of safety, dignity, and delight.

Considered as a complex person, he condescended to act officially on our behalf, as if inferior to Deity. As Mediator he acted under the direction and commission of his Father; and as such, was God's servant, though his Son; therefore said, of himself he could do nothing: not through the want of ability, but being under official obligations to adhere to his Father's directions. Though an ambassador can do nothing of himself, and is bound in duty to act in all things in conformity to his instructions, yet it is not from thence inferable that his nature, ability, or mental powers, are inferior to those of his sovereign; for the limitation is not the effect of personal debility, but of office capacity. The blessed Jesus is therefore not only inferior to God as man, but as Mediator; nevertheless, inferiority in office does not prove, nor imply, inferiority of nature. On the contrary, the errand on which he came was so infinitely important, awful, and arduous, that he could not have discharged his trust without the power and penetration of Deity. Hence he appealed to his works in proof of his divine mission, and as evidences of his filial relation to God, in such a sense as exposed him to the charge of blasphemy, had he not been properly divine. John x. 24—38. His true dignity as a divine person being inferable from what he did, his enemies were inexcusable, because his works sufficiently demonstrated to every honest inquiring mind, who he was, as well as from whence he came: though it was inconsistent with his then state of humiliation and debasement, to allow the glories of divinity to shine forth in their infinite splendor. Hence, he repeatedly charged his friends not to publish to the world who he was, till after his resurrection from the dead. That he was a man, his enemies knew as well as his disciples; yea, some of them thought him to be the promised Messiah, and said one to another, This is the heir, let us kill him: but as a divine person they knew him not; for, had they known him, they would not have crucified the Lord of Glory. For the principal charge brought against him, and for which he was condemned, was, that, being a man, he made himself equal with God. John v. 18, and xix. 7.

If Christ exposed himself to death through ambiguity, how did he witness a good confession at Pilate's bar? If he did not mean an equality with

God, which the Jews thought he did, strange that his regard to truth did not lead to an explanation of what he intended.

It is no wonder that priests and others in that day of prevalent ignorance and perverseness, should have a secret conviction of his office capacity as Messiah, without an idea of his divinity, seeing, some under the profession of gospel ministers, acknowledge and plead for his divine mission, and yet oppose and reject with contempt the idea of his being a divine person.

Consider the complex capacity of Jesus as God, and as man, with his acting as Mediator, in consequence of such an union of distinct natures, and then the Scripture account of his inferiority and subjection to the divine Father will appear quite consonant with the doctrine of his true and proper divinity. But when the aforesaid difficulty is removed, behold another is with equal art thrown in the way of the ignorant and unwary, which is,

2. A perversion of the terms used in treating of this important subject. In consequence of such unwarrantable craft, the *unity* of the divine *essence* is represented to be so evidently inconsistent with a *plurality* of divine *persons,* as if it was universally agreed to consider them as absolute contradictions, and to convey irreconcileable ideas; whereas, it is very well known that those who believe

the divinity of the blessed Jesus, as firmly maintain the unity of the divine essence, or that there is only one God, as they do who oppose a plurality of divine persons. Yet things are represented as if they and the Trinitarians agreed in that about which they differ, and as if they differed about that in which they are agreed. For the consistency between a plurality of *persons* in the one divine *essence,* is the very thing for which those contend who believe the divinity of Christ. And that there is but one living and true God, both parties agree. The doctrines of unity in the divine *essence,* and a plurality of *persons,* are in their very nature distinct, and ought never to be confounded. But that they are opposites has not yet been proved, and I believe never will.

Though the adversaries of Christ's divinity *oppose* the one to the other, as if they were allowed contrarieties; yet, by and by, they will treat those very terms by which the doctrines are distinguished, as if they were intended to convey similar ideas. Hence, if the *essence* of God be the subject treated of, the term *person* is immediately substituted, as if synonymous with that of *essence,* and then with an air of triumph it is inferred, that *If God be one, he is not two or three.* Again, if the doctrine of divine *personality* be the matter of immediate consideration, and scriptural proofs be adduced in support of a plurality of PERSONS truly divine, behold the idea of *essence* is by them substituted in the room of *person*, and *unity* instead of *plurality*, and by the help of such a substitution and perversion of terms, and shuffle of ideas, they very gravely exclaim against Tritheism, i. e., the doctrine of three Gods.

As the friends of Christ's divinity never assert God to be three in the sense in which he is one, nor one in the same sense in which he is three, but perpetually distinguish between a plurality of persons and the unity of God, the methods taken as aforesaid are disingenuous, contemptible, and beneath notice, were it not that thereby inattentive minds are imposed upon.

It is evident, that according to the Scriptures there was a plurality of persons antecedent to creation; for, "in the beginning was the Word, and the word was with God, and the Word was God, the same was in the beginning with God: all things were made by him, and without him, was not any thing made that was made." John i. 1, 2, 3. That glorious person who was *with* God, was, therefore, distinct from him with whom he was, and yet of the same nature, being one in essence with the Father. For the Word was God, and that Jesus Christ is intended by the Word who was in the beginning with God, and the author of creation, is plain from verse 10. "He was in the world, and the world was made by him." Again, verse 14, "The Word was made flesh and dwelt among us, and we beheld his glory, the glory as of the only begotten of the Father, full of grace and truth." "He was before all things, and by him all things consist." Col. i. 17. He was with the Father from everlasting, and all that is done in time is according to the eternal purpose which the Father purposed in him.

Many instances might be given of Christ's existence before his incarnation, as he said, "Before Abraham was, I am." John viii. 58. The plural pronouns used in Scripture by the great Eternal when speaking of acts, authority, and properties peculiar to Deity, are striking proofs of a plurality of persons in one essence. God said, "Let US make man in OUR image, after our likeness." Gen. i. 26. "Behold the man is become as one of US;" chap. iii. 22. "Let US go down and confound their language." chap. xi. 7. "Whom shall I send, and who will go for US?" Isaiah, vi. 8. And respecting all other objects of worship, Jehovah's language is, "Produce your cause, saith the Lord: bring forth your strong reasons, saith the King of Jacob. Let them show the former things what they be, that WE may consider them; or declare US things for to come, that WE may know that ye are gods; yea, do good or do evil, that WE may be dismayed, and behold it together." Isaiah xli. 21, 22, 23. Again, to stain the pride of man and curb human arrogance, he asserts his divine prerogative in the following solemn and instructive interrogations. "Who hath declared from the beginning that WE may know? And *before* time, that WE may say he is righteous? I beheld, and there was no man, no counsellor, that when I asked them could answer a word." Isaiah xli. 26. 28. From those and many more instances which might be produced, it is evident, that there is a plurality of persons in the one eternal God, even the Father, the Word, and the Holy Ghost, and that these three are one. In the name of which sacred three the holy ordinance of baptism was ordered to be administered.

The adversaries of Christ's divinity block up the way leading to the divine glories of Jesus by another stumbling-block, which is,

3. The pre-existence of Christ's soul. Some have maintained this sentiment without any designed injury to the doctrine of the Trinity. But the enemies of Christ's divine personality, find it impossible to give their scheme of opposition even the appearance of consistency, but as aided by the

aforesaid hypothesis; therefore great pains have been taken to render it plausible.

But that it was not a human soul which existed with the Father before time, and which made the world, and to which God spake, saying, Let us make man, will appear, if the following things be duly considered. He who was with the Father, "was with him from everlasting, rejoicing always before him, and whose goings forth have been from of old, from everlasting;" Mic. v. 2; and who should be called, though clothed with humanity "the everlasting Father, the mighty God." Isaiah ix. 6. But it is absurd to suppose a creature to have existed before time began. To suppose a creature always to have been, is to form an idea of a creature which was never created. All things were made by Jesus Christ, without him nothing was made that was made; but according to the aforesaid opinion, there was a creature made which Jesus Christ was no way concerned in the formation of; for a creature cannot be said to have created itself, without absurdly supposing it to have been before it was, to exist prior to its existence, or to act whilst it was nothing, in order to be something. The above absurdities are unavoidable: if the Scripture account of the creation (as the production of a plurality of persons) be credited, and the divinity of Christ be denied.

As a soul could not create itself, so neither could it be the author of the other parts of the creation, which Jesus Christ is positively declared to be. For, "by him were all things created that are in heaven, and that are in earth, visible and invisible, whether they be thrones, or dominions, principalities, or powers: all things were created by him and for him." Col. i. 16. If a human soul be the author of creation, various creatures would be above their Creator. Angels, for instance, would be superior to their Maker, and excel him in strength; for man (which Christ is asserted only to be) is naturally inferior to those celestial spirits. "Thou madest him a little lower than the angels;" which supposes the angels were, when his humanity was made. Heb. ii. 7.

The acknowledgment of Christ as Creator, renders the denial of his proper divinity inexcusable. For, if Jesus be the former of all things, "then the invisible things of him from the creation of the world are clearly seen, being understood by the things that are made, even his eternal power and Godhead, so that they are without excuse who glorify him not as God." Rom. i. 20, 21.

Some assert that Christ was only an instrument in creation; but the work of creation was of such a nature as to exclude the idea of an *instrumental* creator. An instrument must have been employed either *before* or *after* the production of being, for there was no medium. Not *before*, because prior to creation there was not *any thing* existing for an instrument to act upon, or to be employed about. Not *after*, because when a creature *does* exist, it is too late for an instrument to be employed in producing it. Nothing short of infinite agency could possibly be concerned in creation; the persons so engaged were properly divine, and essentially one. However, that there was no instrument concerned is beyond all dispute, if what Jehovah says be duly regarded; for he declares there was none such with him. Prov. viii.; Mic. v. 2. "Thus saith the Lord thy Redeemer, and he that formed thee from the womb; I am the Lord that maketh all things, that stretcheth forth the heavens ALONE, that spreadeth abroad the earth BY MYSELF." Isaiah xliv. 24. "Who ALONE spreadeth out the heavens." Job ix. 8. Hence it appears, that though there were distinct persons employed in creation, yet they were so united as to be included in the one all-creating Jehovah.

4. To render the idea of the soul existing before time, instead of the Son of God, less exceptionable; it has been thought proper to exclude the body from being an essential constituent part of a man. Such an exclusion to be sure was a happy thought, and quite necessary; for without

it the all-creating creature would not have been properly either *God*, *angel*, or *man*. But that it might be considered as belonging to some scale or class of being, it is asserted to be "a proper human person, a true and real man, the body being only a temporary covering for, but not a constituent part of, human nature."

This method of depreciating the divine glories of the blessed Jesus will prove abortive, if the Scripture account of human nature be attended to. From the sacred pages we learn, that the Lord God formed *man* of the dust of the ground, and breathed into his nostrils the breath of life, and *man* became a living soul; Gen. ii. 7: and that the rib, which the Lord God had taken from man, made he a woman! and Adam said, she shall be called woman, because she was taken *out* of *man*. Again, to Adam as a transgressor, the Lord said, "Dust thou art, and unto dust shalt thou return." Gen. iii. 19. Man shall return again to dust. Now as the soul was not formed of the dust, nor the rib of which Eve was made, taken out of the *soul;* but the rib from the body, and the body from the ground; therefore, the body must be a constituent part of man, for the body only returns to dust, and yet the Lord says, *man* shall return thither. Job xxxiv. 15.

Again, the personal name of man is often given

to the body, which would be improper if the body was not a part of the person. Jacob in his affecting lamentation says, "Joseph is without doubt rent in pieces. I will go down into the grave unto my son mourning." Gen. xxxvii. 33. 35. It was not the *soul*, but the *body* of his son which he concluded was torn asunder; nor his own soul, but his body, that would go down to the grave. And when the same patriarch was near death, he charged his sons, saying, "Bury me with my fathers;" in such a cave which he described; adding, "there they buried *Abraham* and *Sarah* his wife; there they buried *Isaac* and *Rebekah* his wife, and there I buried Leah." Gen. xlix. 29, 31.

And that the body of Christ was an essential part of his humanity, is evident from what the angel said to his weeping friends. "*He is not here, he is risen:* Come, see the place where the Lord lay." Matt. xxviii. 6. But if the body was no proper constituent part of his manhood, he never lay in the grave; nor did he ever rise from the dead, for he did not die. They did not nail *him* to the tree; the whole account of his bodily sufferings is a mere fiction, if it be true, that his body was not a proper constituent part of himself. In a word, there never will be a resurrection of any man, if *bodies* are not essential to human nature, and this world of men are quite as invisible to each other as the world of angels are to them. According to that notion, the sight of a man is a singular rarity. That a soul can exist without a body is readily allowed, but such a separate existence is the effect of *death;* and can it be thought reasonable that Christ's first existence should be a state similar to that of the dead?

Once more, on such a supposition Christ could not be the son of man in any sense, because his soul is said to exist before all men; and his body not a part of his humanity. But he was the son of David, a descendant of Abraham, as the Scriptures assert, and as the apostle to the Hebrews said, "It is evident that our Lord sprang out of Judah." Heb. vii. 14.

To conclude; the incarnation of Christ was not only considered by the great apostle as an instance of infinite condescension, but admired by him and every believer in his day, as being in its nature really inexplicable, and truly mysterious; they did not dispute the fact, though they could not conceive *how* divinity and humanity were united in one person; but rejoiced in its reality as a pillar and ground of the truth. "Without controversy, great is the mystery of godliness: God was manifest in the flesh." 1 Tim. iii. 15, 16. "The Word" which "was God," "was made flesh, and dwelt amongst us."

But if Christ be only a man, or a mere creature, the wonder ceases, for it cannot be thought a thing singular and surprising for a human soul to possess a body; nor for God to manifest himself to a holy creature, and employ in his service a good man. It is truly lamentable and really astonishing that any who wish to be saved by Jesus, should endeavor to sink his character and diminish his dignity: yea, rejoice in hope of proving the Saviour infinitely unworthy of their supreme love and delight. You, happy souls, who need, know, and esteem the Redeemer, as infinitely powerful, and precious—Oh, pity the condition of such, whose peace and pleasure rise *high* in consequence of the Saviour *sinking low* in their esteem. Pray for them, and take heed lest you also be tempted; and labor that your own faith may be firm, and your love fervent toward the infinitely glorious and lovely Redeemer. Consider and frequently contemplate the proofs of his proper divinity, as recorded in the sacred volume: such as the properties of which he is possessed, the work he has performed, the worship he has received from angels and men, the divine names and titles which are given him, the honors ascribed to him, the unlimited confidence placed in him by good men in every age, and the claims which are made by him; for he, who was never the subject of arrogance, "thought it not robbery to be equal with God." Phil. ii. 6. The Lord grant that every reader may search the Scriptures which testify of Jesus, with godly sincerity and gospel simplicity. "To the upright, light shall arise in darkness."

CHAPTER II.

DIFFICULTIES CONCERNING THE LOVE OF GOD.

THAT Jehovah changeth not, is a self-evident truth, a scripture axiom. "With him there is no variableness, nor shadow of turning." Being perfection itself, therefore the properties of his nature, and purposes of his will, are absolutely unalterable. What he has determined, shall be done. "He is of one mind, and who can turn him? For the counsel of the Lord standeth forever, the thoughts of his heart to all generations, and to Zion he says, he will rest in his love. He will rejoice over her with singing; for having loved his own which were in the world, he loved them unto the end." Notwithstanding the above and such like solemn declarations made by the God of truth, such objections have been raised against the unchangeableness of Jehovah's love, as greatly to perplex and stumble some who are evidently the objects of it.

God could not produce creatures morally defective, or disagreeable to himself; they were what he willed them to be, i. e. *good*, yea, *very good*, and as such were loved and delighted in, by their Maker. Every creature being Jehovah's production, therefore no creature was, in its original state, the object of his disapprobation. Yet many of them are now the declared objects of his hatred and indignation. From these self-evident facts, it is inferred by some sincere inquirers after truth, that the love of God is changeable, and not invariably fixed on its objects; which inference has perplexed many of the people of God, and proved a stumbling-block in their way. From this source various errors have proceeded, by which the glorious gospel of the grace of God has been beclouded, the faith of many Christians staggered, and their joy in Jesus and hope of glory greatly diminished.

The love of God, according to the Scriptures, ought to be considered under the distinctions, of NATURAL and as SOVEREIGN. The righteous Lord loveth righteousness, and holiness is his perpetual delight. This love arises from the perfection and purity of his nature, and has for its object his own holy image, as stamped upon his rational creatures. In other words, in holy dispositions and corresponding acts, the Lord takes pleasure and delight. He is of purer eyes than to behold iniquity with approbation, or look on holiness with disgust. His hatred of sin, and love of purity, are not acts of sovereignty. Sin is not hateful because God willed it should be so, but is odious in its own nature to every pure being; and is therefore infinitely hateful to an infinitely holy God.

God does not hate sin, because he has by his law forbidden it; but has forbidden it, because it is what he loathes, as contrary to his holy nature. Perfect conformity to God, and supreme delight in him as the chief good, are enforced by God's holy law, because of their native excellence and propriety. Holiness then, being the object of God's *natural* love, or essential approbation, and sin the reverse, it necessarily follows that every unholy creature is odious in the sight of God; therefore a creature having lost its purity, ceases to be the object of his natural approbation; yet the alteration is not in God, but in the creature, which is become, through moral impurity, what he abhors. God's love is still unalterably fixed on personal purity, wherever it is found; but in reference to a polluted creature, love has lost its object, that on which it was fixed being destroyed.

Thus it appears that the various ranks of intelligent creatures were, in their original condition, interested in God's favor. Even those abominable beings, called devils, were, while holy, the objects of their Maker's love and approbation, as well as the angels who continue to shine in holy splendor and purity. Though a part of the angelic world, and the whole human race, have, by their revolt from God, become vile, and cease to be the objects of the Lord's delight, yet there is no variableness or change in Jehovah. To every proper object, "God is love;" 1 John iv. 16; for God has no aversion to his creatures, simply as creatures; but on account of their moral depravity; nor does he necessarily love them, because they owe their existence to his sovereign will and power; but as the subjects of his moral image, which consists in righteousness and true holiness. As all mankind have lost the image of God in which they were created, and become base and abominable in his sight, being filthy and guilty before him, they must have continued in a condition eternally disgustful to God, and in a state tremendously terrible to themselves, had not the Lord been pleased to show them kindness in a sovereign way; being graciously determined to save whom he thought proper, with an everlasting salvation. That love from which salvation springs is not *natural* but *sovereign;* not *necessary* but absolutely *free.* None are its objects because they deserved to be so, nor was God under any necessity of nature so to distinguish them; but it consisted in a voluntary determination to do good to the persons he sovereignly fixed upon as his people, with infinite and invariable delight.

If, then, we consider the *voluntary love* of the great Eternal as distinct from, and yet harmonizing with, that *natural* and *necessary* love of which we have been treating, difficulties, otherwise insurmountable, will disappear. That love which is *essential,* or natural to God, has personal holiness or pure principles for its invariable object. But *sovereign* love fixed upon persons without a regard had to their dispositions as its cause; which sovereign favor is entirely uninfluenced by their dispositions, and is beautifully illustrated by the Lord's voluntary favor to the person of Jacob, and the distinguished special privileges enjoyed by his posterity, without respect had to his having done either good or evil. "Jacob have I loved, saith the Lord." Rom. ix. 13.* And Moses, speaking of Israel as a chosen people, observes, The Lord did not set his love upon you, nor choose you because ye were more in number

* The hatred of Esau, as opposed to the love of the Lord to Jacob, is not to be considered as implying any positive indignation to his person as a sinner; because the love and the hatred spoken of, was without their having done either good or evil; it only intends his *not being loved* as Jacob was. In this sense, hatred is to be understood in Deut. xxi. 15; Luke xxiv. 26; John xii. 25, &c.

than any people, (for ye were the fewest of all people,) but because the Lord loved you. Deut. vii. 7, 8. Such as it hath pleased the Lord to make his people, 1 Sam. xii. 22, may with humble joy and holy admiration say, "Behold what manner of love the Father hath bestowed upon us, that we should be called the sons of God." 1 John iii. 1. This sovereign love of the Lord to his spiritual Israel, set apart his own son, Immanuel, as the head of his people, and gave their persons to him before the world was; and in time gave him to die for them. God loved their persons, but abhorring their sinful conduct and criminal dispositions, was determined to remove that from them which he hated in them, and by creating them anew in Christ Jesus, or implanting holy and heavenly principles in their souls, to make them a holy people, that as such they might become the suitable, fit, and proper objects of his natural, necessary, and essential love. Sovereign love having their persons only for its objects, without being excited by their dispositions, is therefore invariably the same, without addition or diminution. Hence all that is done for them, and wrought in them, is in consequence of, and according to that great love wherewith he loved them, even when they were dead in trespasses and sins. This sovereign love is the fruit of God's good pleasure. The utility and propriety of the above distinction, were it sufficiently attended to, would appear as bright as the sun in a clear meridian. I wish some able pen would undertake to investigate the subject more fully than either my talents or time will admit of. However, the few following remarks I hope may be of use to weak Christians, for whose sake I write, either to rectify their judgments, stimulate their obedience, increase their joy, or relieve their perplexity.

1. From the sacred oracles it appears, that God's necessary hatred to sin is not contrary to his sovereign love or gracious intentions to do good to his people, even while they are subjects of no other dispositions than what he abhors. If sovereign love to the sinner was inconsistent with his infinite hatred to sin, who then could be saved? Fallen men are, as such, altogether abominable in the eyes of their holy Maker, the imagination of their hearts being, while unrenewed, evil, only evil, and that continually. "They are corrupt, they have done abominable works, there is none that doeth good, no, not one;" Psal. xiv. 1, 3; compared with Rom. iii. 9, 18. "We ourselves also, were sometimes foolish, disobedient, deceived, serving divers lusts and pleasures, living in malice and envy, hateful and hating one another." Tit. iii. 3. They who do such things are worthy of

death, and likewise those who take pleasure in them that do them. Rom. i. 32. "So then they that are in the flesh cannot please God." Rom. viii. 8. Nevertheless, "God commendeth his love towards us, in that, while we were yet sinners Christ died for us." Rom. v. 8. "Herein is love, not that we loved God, but that he loved us, and sent his Son to be the propitiation for our sins." 1 John iv. 10. "In this was the love of God manifest." Ver. 9. "Yea, I have loved thee with an everlasting love: therefore with loving kindness have I drawn thee." Jer. xxxi. 3. Jesus when pleading with his Father, on behalf of his chosen, says, "Thou hast loved them as thou hast loved me, and thou lovedst me before the foundation of the world." John xvii. 23, 24. "We all had our conversation in times past in the lust of our flesh, fulfilling the desires of the flesh and of the mind, and were by nature the children of wrath, even as others. But God, who is rich in mercy, for his great love wherewith he loved us, even when we were dead in sins, hath quickened us, &c." Eph. ii. 3, 4, 5. "After that the kindness and love of God our Saviour appeared toward man; not by works of righteousness which we have done, but according to his mercy he saved us, by the washing of regeneration, and renewing of the Holy Ghost." Tit. iii. 5. Being thus the workmanship

5

of God created anew in Christ, the church becomes the object of the Lord's necessary love, or natural delight. As he saith, "I will call her beloved which was not beloved." Rom. ix. 25.

2. Those who are renewed in the spirit of their minds, and possessed of holy principles, and are undeniably, as such, the objects of God's natural love, may through sin, become the objects of his holy displeasure. Nevertheless, that does not suppose, nor imply any change in Jehovah. Not in his sovereign good will, which has regard to their persons, and which is still the same, being the effect of his mere good pleasure, and not fixed on them because of any good moral quality in them. Nor is there any change in his natural love, because only holiness is its invariable object. Agreeably to, and in proof of the above, we read that though God *loved*, yet he greatly *abhorred* Israel, and was wroth with his inheritance. Ps. lxxviii. 59. 62. Being defiled with their own works, "therefore was the wrath of the Lord kindled against his people, insomuch that he abhorred his own inheritance." Ps. cvi. 40. "Nevertheless, he regarded them when he heard their cry;" ver. 44. "Yea, mine heritage, saith the Lord, is unto me as a lion in the forest, it crieth out against me, therefore *I hate* it. I *hate* the *dearly beloved* of my soul." Jer. xii. 7, 8. "Thou hast wearied

me with thine iniquities;" yet sovereign grace breaks forth in Israel's favor, and Jehovah adds, "I, even I, am he that blotteth out thy transgressions for mine own sake, and will not remember thy sins." Isaiah xliii. 24, 25.

3. Of that love which is essential to the nature of God, good men are not equally the objects; for as no man is its object but in consequence of being the subject of holiness, therefore, a growth in grace, or in holy obedience, will ever meet with God's increasing approbation. Christ, as man, though ever pure, "increased in favor with God." Luke ii. 52. "Therefore doth my Father love me because I lay down my life." John x. 17. "He that loveth me shall be loved of my Father, and I will love him. If a man love me, he will keep my words, and my Father will love him, and we will come unto him, and make our abode with him." John xiv. 21, 23. "For the Father himself loveth you, *because* ye have loved me, and have believed that I came out from God." John xvi. 27. "Keep yourselves in the love of God." Jude, 21st verse. "As the Father hath loved me, so have I loved you; continue ye in my love. If ye keep my commandments, ye shall abide in my love, even as I have kept my Father's commandments and abide in his love." John xv. 9, 10. Though all regenerate persons are evidently the

equal objects of special sovereign favor, and with them, as in Christ, the Lord is well pleased for his righteousness' sake, and their persons are accepted in the beloved; yet with many of them the Lord is not well pleased, with respect to the temper of their hearts, and manner of life. See 1 Cor. x. 4, 5. Therefore, "only let your conversation be as becometh the gospel of Christ." "We beseech you, brethren, and exhort you by the Lord Jesus Christ, that as ye have received of us how ye ought to walk, and to *please* God, so ye would abound more and more." Phil. i. 2; 71 Thess. iv. 1. "Knowing that your labor shall not be in vain in the Lord." 1 Cor. xv. 58. "For God is not unrighteous to forget your work and labor of love." Heb. vi. 10.* From the above we may infer:

1. That the everlasting damnation of those who kept not their first estate in which they enjoyed

---

* The meaning of the excellent author, may perhaps be more lucidly and connectedly presented thus: No man is the object of God's *natural* love, unless he is the subject of *holiness;* for holiness is the proper and only object of his love; and every man is thus beloved of God in *proportion* to the degree in which he is holy: but the children of God are holy in a great variety of degrees; they are, therefore, in the same variety of degrees, the objects of God's natural love.

J. A. W.

the Divine approbation,* does not oppose the unchangeable nature of Jehovah's love, nor render the eternal salvation of his people precarious or uncertain.

2. How carefully should every saint watch against every sin, and strive to grow in perfect conformity to his God. True happiness will ever be found inseparably connected with real holiness; and sin, wherever it is, will invariably remain the object of God's displeasure. On the account of this he hides his face, and is wroth with his people; and though he pardon them, yet he will take vengeance on their inventions; for whom he loveth he chasteneth.

3. How awfully miserable must our condition have been, having lost that rectitude of nature in which God delighted, had he not proceeded to-

* That approbation was his *natural*, and not his *sovereign* love: its object was their *disposition*, i. e., holiness, and not their *persons*. But this disposition they no longer possess; hence, he can no longer love it in them: yet the change is not in him, but in them. But his people the Lord loves with a *sovereign* love; the object of this love is their *persons*, irrespective of their dispositions. Change, then, in their dispositions (as when they backslide) effects no change in *sovereign* love; for it takes no cognizance of dispositions. Yet, as we have seen above, it deprives them of God's *natural* love; for their sin is a removal of their holiness which is *its* proper object. J. A. W.

wards us in a way of sovereign grace, choosing us in, and committing our persons to the care of his own Son, laying our iniquities upon him, and justifying us on his account, conveying holiness, pardon and peace, through him, to make us pure and spotless before his throne! There, in that world of bliss, God, in all his essential glories, will be forever enjoyed the same as though sin had never been; with additional pleasures arising from the amazing infinite source of sovereign spontaneous favor. The hearts of the redeemed will be ravished, their powers of mind animated, and their elevated songs make heaven's high arches ring with the joyful acclamation of, *Salvation to our God and the Lamb.* A full evidence of the infinite desert of sin, which seems to be intended by the smoke of the furnace ascending before the throne, will heighten their admiration of sovereign love, and fill their capacious souls with unspeakable joy, profound reverence, and holy wonder.

4. Opposition to the sovereign grace of God is truly lamentable. How mournful to think that poor condemned criminals should be filled with enmity against that, in consequence of which, only, salvation can become the object of hope. It is a striking proof of the deceitful and infatuating nature of sin, and the pride of the human heart.

CHAPTER III.

THE DOCTRINE OF ELECTION.

ELECTION or choice always implies freedom of will in the persons who choose or elect. Constraint or compulsion is opposite to choice, which must be voluntary or not at all.

Every elector has an end in view, in respect of which he makes his choice, or for the accomplishment of which the choice is made.

The person chosen is always considered as passive, being entirely at the will of the elector, so far as relates to the act of choosing.

These three ideas are inseparably connected with election, whatever kind of election we refer to, whether made by God or man. But some Christians have confused or discouraging ideas of the doctrine now under consideration, for the want of attending to the different senses in which the Scriptures speak of persons being the chosen, or the elect of God. Of this ignorance or inattention the opposers of sovereign grace take the advantage; and in order to perplex or prejudice their minds, produce Scripture instances of some who were *elected*, and nevertheless perished in their sins, as there is reason to think Saul and Judas did, and yet both of them were chosen of God. Hence it is inferred, that as some are lost who were elected, therefore election does not secure the salvation of those who are chosen, but is of such a nature as to leave their future happiness entirely precarious.

But the apostle exhorts Christians to give all diligence to make their calling and election sure, by being able to produce such evidences as may demonstrate their personal interest in Jehovah's choice: the knowledge of which, in the judgment of Jesus, is calculated to produce in his people greater pleasure than they ought to take from the evidence of devils being in subjection to them. To have hell vanquished must afford unutterable joy to those who wrestle with the powers of darkness; "notwithstanding in this rejoice not, that the spirits are subject unto you, but rather rejoice because your names are written in heaven." Luke x. 20.

For the relief of serious inquirers after truth, it may be proper to observe, that by Election, in Scripture, is sometimes intended God's setting apart, or choosing a people, to the enjoyment of peculiar external privileges; in that sense he chose the Jewish nation, and, therefore, they, as a nation, notwithstanding their wickedness, are frequently called the Lord's elect, or chosen people. Again, the Lord hath elected, or chosen, particular persons to act in office capacity; as Samuel, Saul, David, and many more under the Old Testament; and Peter, James, Judas, and others, were chosen, or elected in like manner under the New. Hence, Jesus said to his disciples, "Have not I chosen you twelve? and one of you is a devil."

But the election of grace, of which I am treating, is of a different nature, and consists in God's choosing persons in Christ Jesus, or setting them apart as in connexion with him, to salvation, through sanctification of the Spirit, and belief of the truth. Salvation was the end God had in view;—to bring his chosen to the possession and enjoyment of *salvation*, not only as consisting in a deliverance from punishment, but from all iniquity. Therefore, in the definition the apostle gives of the doctrine, sanctification by the Spirit, and a true faith, were what these persons were chosen to be the subjects of, through which only, salvation could be enjoyed. This choice was from the beginning, or ever the earth was. They were not chosen, because they were viewed as holy, and deserving to be God's favorites, on account of their obedience or personal purity, but that they *should* be holy. The great apostle, in his deep, but delightful epistle to the saints at Ephesus, treats of the important subject in so full, plain, and accurate a manner, as to answer almost every pertinent query that can be made respecting the doctrine. He begins with expressions of fervid affection and humble gratitude to its infinite Author, saying, "Blessed be the God and Father of our Lord Jesus Christ."

Q. What hath he done?

A. "Who hath blessed us."

Q. With what hath he blessed us?

A. "With all spiritual blessings."

Q. Where are those blessings deposited?

A. "In Christ."

Q. Where may seeking souls expect to find and enjoy them?

A. "In heavenly places" (or things.)

Q. According to what does he proceed in the bestowment of such special privileges: is it owing to our choice of him?

A. No; but "according as he hath chosen us in him."

Q. When?

A. "Before the foundation of the world."

Q. But did he choose us because we were holy, or because he foresaw we would be so?

A. No; but "that we *should* be holy."

Q. Did he then intend that all such should be made completely holy?

A. Yes, and "without blame before him in love."

Q. And is every thing aforesaid absolutely secured?

A. Yes, having predestinated us.

Q, Predestinated to what?

A. "Unto the adoption of children."

Q. By, and to whom?

A. "By Jesus Christ himself."

Q. What is the source of such favors, or from whence do they flow?

A. "The good pleasure of his will."

Q. In what does the whole terminate, or to what does it lead?

A. "To the praise of the glory of his grace." "Wherein he hath made us accepted in the Beloved, in whom we have redemption through his blood, the forgiveness of sins according to the riches of his grace." See Eph. i. 4th to the 12th. Again, the same inspired writer asserts, such were "chosen to salvation, through sanctification of the Spirit and belief of the truth." 2 Thess. ii. 13. God kindly connected their final felicity and his own eternal glory, when he ordained them to eternal life. Acts xiii. 48. But though Judas was chosen to office, he was not chosen to holiness, for Jesus, when speaking to the disciples as his servants and true followers, (Judas being present,) he said, "I speak not of you all. I know whom I have chosen." John xiii. 18. The names of his chosen are written in heaven, and all such are freed from condemnation. "Who shall lay any thing to the charge of God's elect?" Rom. viii. 33. All this could not with propriety be said of the Jewish nation, nor of Judas, and many more who have been chosen merely to office: besides, individuals are called the elect, who could not bear rule in the church of God; for a woman was not suffered to speak in the church, nor to usurp authority over the man, but was to be in silence. 1 Tim. ii. 12. Yet we read of an elect lady and her elect sister. 2 John i. 13. If God hath thus chosen, the end he had in view will certainly be accomplished, for saith Jesus, "All that the Father giveth me shall come unto me, and him that cometh unto me I will in no wise cast out." "His people shall be willing in the day of his power," for having "loved them with an everlasting love, therefore, with loving kindness will he draw them." No one instance can be given of God having chosen any *people*, *person*, or *place*, to that which was not actually accomplished. Did the Lord choose the Jewish nation to peculiar privileges? Yes, and in consequence of that choice they had the advantage of all other nations, and much every way. Samuel did actually prophecy, and Saul and David were really kings in Israel. Judas was actually numbered with the apostles, and with them took part of the *ministry* to which he was elected. Moses was Israel's leader, and lawgiver, because he was chosen by the Lord to such dignity. Aaron and his descendants were priests of the most high God, because they were *elected* by him to that office. So the Lord chose Jerusalem as the residence of the *ark*, and the place where sacrifices should be offered; and thither the tribes of Israel actually repaired to worship, and adore him whose dwelling was in Zion. In no one instance did Jehovah choose in vain. The ends he had in view were ever accomplished. And if so, can there be any reason assigned why those, and those only who were chosen to the greatest blessings, should fall short of them? But "the foundation standeth sure, having this seal, the Lord knoweth them that are his." In every age "as many as were ordained to eternal life believed," "the election obtained it, but the rest were blinded" by "the god of this world, who blindeth the eyes of them who believe not." "So then at this present time also there is a remnant according to the election of grace, and if by grace, then it is no more of works, otherwise grace is no more grace." Rom. xi. 5, 6.

Another stumbling-block in the way of many inquirers, next to the doctrine of election, is *reprobation*, which is generally but improperly considered as the counterpart of election, and related to it as its direct opposite; as a negative, is related to a positive idea. But if it be understood as the negative of election, is it not strange it should change its nature, and, in controversy, become a positive idea? And yet as such it has been both opposed and defended with great warmth; for the adversaries of sovereign grace scarcely ever directly encounter the doctrine of election; but artfully file off to reprobation, as if they were conscious that election was itself invulnerable, and could not possibly be reduced. But from the mountain of reprobation they attack the doctrine intended to be demolished, and charge it with the most horrid consequences. These consequences the defenders of sovereign grace have repeatedly proved to be not in the least inferable from the doctrine of God's sovereign choice of his people to grace and glory. But perhaps their defence of the doctrine of reprobation has not been equally successful. And no wonder;—they have unwarily admitted it to be the opposite of election; and this admission has been stumbling to many inquirers after truth, and encouraging to its opposers. Election or choice, indeed, implies a negative, or that some are not chosen; which the Scripture calls the *rest:* this is readily allowed, but reprobation as mentioned in Scripture is never opposed to election. To the doctrine of election it does not seem related, but stands in a quite different situation in the system of scriptural divinity.

1. If reprobation conveyed the idea of non-election, by a person being reprobated, we should understand one not elected; but how will such an idea comport with the apostle's reasoning, when he says, "Know ye not that Jesus Christ is in you except ye be reprobates?" 2 Cor. xv. 15. To suppose him to mean they were not elected if Christ was not in them, is supposing him to contradict his own experience, and oppose self-evident facts; for there was a time when Christ was not in Paul himself; during which period he was exceeding mad against those who professed the name of Jesus. "But," says he, "it pleased God to reveal his Son in me." Before this happy change took place he was in a state of reprobation, for Christ was not in him, and yet he was never in a state of *non-election,* but was one chosen in Christ before the world was. Again, he could not mean if Christ was not in them they were not

elected, because Christ is not naturally in his elect, as most of them know; and they lament, when called by grace, that they lived without God and without Christ in the world; therefore, during that period, they were *reprobates*, not having Christ in them; nevertheless they were the elect of God, of which their being called by grace is a proof. From hence it appears that reprobation is not the opposite of election.

2. That reprobation is not the opposite of election will appear evident, if it be considered that election is an act of divine sovereignty, arising merely from the will of God, without any fitness in creatures deserving to be so distinguished; but reprobation, whenever the word is used in Scripture, respects a comparative deficiency, or an essential defect in those who are reprobated. Election is the effect of, or entirely flows from the good pleasure of God's will in favor of the *persons* of his people; but reprobation originates not merely from God's will, but from the natural contrariety there is between Jehovah's purity and their pollution.*

---

* If the distinction laid down, page 48, between the love of God as Natural and as Sovereign be borne in mind, it will render even more clear, the point which the author is here discussing. Election is the choice which *sovereign love* makes of the *persons* of such as shall be saved. But Reprobation is

3. Reprobation in Scripture always stands opposed to, and is the natural negative of, approbation, whether it respect the state of a person, the frame of his mind, or the nature of his actions. Hence, vile professors are compared to the alloy or dross frequently mixed with metal. Therefore "reprobate silver shall men call them, because the LORD has rejected them." Jer. vi. 30. "Know ye not that Christ is in you except ye be reprobates?" the apostle's obvious meaning is, that such are destitute of real worth. However splendid a profession be, yet without Christ, all will be found mere refuse at last; therefore he puts them upon close examination, lest they should be deceived by appearances, "thinking themselves something, while they are nothing." Hence in the next verse he adds, "I trust that ye shall

not the opposite of this;—it is God's *natural* aversion to the *disposition* (i. e. the *unholiness*) of sinners, whether elect or not. And as God's *natural* hatred to the *disposition* of an impenitent sinner would be no proof that the *person* of the same sinner was not an object of his *sovereign* love, so, neither is the fact that a man is *reprobate*, any proof that he is *not elect;* for as God "loved" Israel with a *sovereign* love, and yet "greatly abhorred" them with a *natural* aversion, (Psal. lxxviii. 59, comp. 62,) and this love and abhorrence were not only compatible, but co-existent; so are the election and reprobation (i. e. disapproval; see following section) of the same person compatible, and may be co-existent, and, therefore, one cannot be the opposite of the other. J. A. W.

know that we are not reprobates; 2 Cor. xiii. 5, 6; and in verse 7, he says, "I pray to God that ye do no evil, not that we should appear *approved*, but that ye should do that which is honest, though we be as *reprobates.*" Thus he considers reprobation and approbation as natural opposites. Again, men of *corrupt* minds are said to be "reprobate concerning the faith," i. e. destitute of a true understanding of the truth. 2 Tim. iii. 8. And the "abominable and disobedient are unto every good work reprobate." Tit. i. 16.

Agreeable, therefore, to this view of reprobation, those vile affections to which the Gentiles were given up, are called "a reprobate mind." Rom. i. 26, 28, 29. Meaning that their dispositions and conduct were odious, and could not possibly be approved of, either by God or good men. From the above considerations it is evident that election and reprobation are not inseparably connected, nor even so much as related as *kindred* ideas, and that reprobation does not intend an appointment to eternal misery, for such may still find mercy as Paul did; but that is the opposite to divine approbation, whether it respect persons, principles, or proceedings.

But some may reply, Though the term reprobation should be disused as relating to election, yet if the ideas be retained which were conveyed by it, the doctrine is not less exceptionable than before. True; therefore let us calmly consider whether those horrid ideas, which the opposers of election have always connected with the term reprobation, are not as foreign to the doctrine of election as the term itself. The sober opposers of the doctrine in question, generally charge it with implying three things: 1. An appointment to inevitable destruction of those who are not elected; therefore, 2. That the doctrine of election is injurious to those not included in it; and consequently, 3. Is a reflection on the justice or moral character of God. These reasons, it is confessed, if well founded, would be quite sufficient to justify a dissent from the doctrine, or an opposition to it. But whether these awful inferences are the genuine offspring of election let us now examine.

1. The first objection is, Whether election be an appointment of any creature to destruction? That it was neither the cause nor the occasion of such an appointment is demonstrably evident from its very nature. It could not have such a tendency, because election is an act absolutely sovereign, or a gracious act arising simply from Jehovah's will. But punishment does not arise from divine sovereignty. If it did, it would be *causeless!* God never punished (therefore never intended to do so)

without a criminal cause in the creature. God does not punish for sin because it was his sovereign will; but his very will to punish arises from the holiness of his nature and the equity of his government; therefore God's intention to punish arises from a *distinct* source from that out of which election springs. They are in their nature as eternally distinct, as any acts of God can possibly be.*

Such a charge therefore might as well be brought against creation as election. It seems very strange that any serious person should oppose the idea of God's decreeing to punish for sin, seeing he actually does so, which he could not, if it was an unrighteous thing. If it be right for the Lord to punish, it could not be wrong to resolve to do so, unless it be wrong to determine to do what is right. However, such a decree does not arise from election. What is opposite to election, is a mere negation, or a leaving others in that state in which all men are viewed by the great Eternal when he chose his people.

2. If election respected its objects as *sinless*, those from among whom they were chosen could

* These distinctions may be thus shown :—The "source" of election is *mercy*. Eph. ii. 4, 5. That of punishment is *justice*. Luke xxiii. 41. The "nature" of the two acts is also distinct:—election is a *gracious* act. Rom. xi. 5. Punishment is a *righteous* one. Rom. iii. 5. J. A. W.

not be deemed punishable, being considered in their pure unfallen state; therefore election, if so considered, could not in the nature of things, be the *cause* or *occasion* of God's designing to punish any man. If election be considered as a choice of *criminal* creatures, or of creatures considered as in a sinful fallen state, in which light it is viewed by many, because the choice is "unto salvation through sanctification of the spirit," (however, the different stating of the doctrine is only a circumstance which does not alter the *nature* of the truth stated, for if it be thus considered,) it unavoidably follows, that as those *not* included in the sovereign choice, were viewed by God as sinful when the choice was made; therefore the choice could not possibly *make* them sinful nor *cause* them to be viewed as criminals. It is absurd to suppose the prescience of God to be the fruit of his sovereign will; and yet this absurdity attends this objection, which is the same as saying, if God had not elected some, he would never have known or thought of the condition of others. As no injury is done to any man by the doctrine in question, therefore,

3. It is not contrary to the moral character of God. In election there is no connivance at sin implied. By it, sin in the chosen was not rendered less odious, nor justice partially administered in their favour, but a surety was graciously substi-

tuted in their stead, who bore their sins, and was wounded for their transgressions, and by whose obedience the law of God was magnified, and through his death impartial justice shone with tremendous lustre.

Had the crimes of which the elect were guilty been transferred or imputed to those who perish, an exemption of the elect from punishment would have been unjust and injurious, because mercy shown to them would have heightened the misery of others. But as every one who perishes suffers only according to the demerit of his own personal sins, therefore to infer that the doctrine of election is detrimental to man, and unworthy of God, discovers either pitiable weakness, or powerful prejudice. Such inferences seem as opposite to truth, decency and common sense, as if we undertook to prove that God is cruel because he is kind, and that those have great cause to complain who were never injured.*

*The following is a condensed view of the doctrine of election.

1. There is a manifest difference among mankind in their moral and religious character;—a difference which is not merely external, but apparently, *radical* and essential: some are the subjects of real, vital piety, of which others are entirely destitute.

2. As every effect must originate in some cause, so this difference in men's characters is an effect of some cause, and the

Scriptures attribute it to God; Eph. ii. 3, 5: "We were by nature children of wrath even as others; but *God—hath quickened us.*"

3. As God is the author of this difference, he has, doubtless, in producing it, acted like an intelligent and wise being. But such a Being does not act until he has *determined* to act; and each act is part of a plan of operation: therefore, before God produced this difference in men's characters, he determined to produce it, and the change produced, is part of his great plan of operations; i. e. what he has done in time, he has resolved to do before time began: he determined, then, to effect the very change he has effected, and in the very persons in whom he has effected it; (Rom. viii. 29, 30;) and this determination is election.

From this it will be seen that election has absolutely *no bearing* upon any but the saved; it does not touch, or *at all* regard others; no more than if they had not any being. It leaves them exactly as they were, and as they would have been if there had been no election at all.

From an inspection of the passage just referred to, in connection with the above remarks, it will be seen, also, that so far from election securing the salvation of any, irrespective of character and piety, their *character* is one object regarded in their election; and election secures that it shall be holy. Eph. i. 4. Election, as we have seen, was the determination that there *should be a difference* in conduct and character between its objects and others; and that they should be sanctified in spirit, by the belief of the truth. 2 Thes. ii. 13.

J. A. W.

CHAPTER IV.

UNION TO CHRIST.

THOUGH the Scriptures speak with remarkable plainness of the near relation subsisting between Christ and his church, in consequence of electing love, yet various stumbling-blocks are frequently found in the way of those who desire clear views of that doctrine; for the removal of which, if God please to bless the attempt, let us now briefly consider that relation to Christ, which is expressed by the title of the present chapter.

Warm disputes have existed among the people of God about union to Christ, particularly as relating to its commencement, which is thought by some to have been from everlasting, and by others not till, or after believing. Though agreed in the main about its nature and duration, each side has been pretty free, and fertile in the invention of consequences, as arising from their opponents' sentiments, which consequences, perhaps, are equally abhorrent to both. On this account, many sincere inquirers after truth have been greatly discouraged, and prevented making progress in religious attainments. Some are also perplexed by a third party, who, differing from the other about the nature of the union, therefore deny its durability, and maintain that those who are in *Christ to-day* may possibly be in hell to-morrow.

Perhaps the doctrine of union with Christ may be of such a copious and complex nature, as to justify in some measure the sentiment of *each*, who, viewing the subject in *detached* parts only, may conclude that some things are *opposite*, which are only *distinct*.

It should be considered, that union to Christ is of a threefold nature, which may (for the sake of keeping ideas distinct) be denominated, *visible*, *vital*, and *virtual*.

First. By *visible*, is intended a credible profession of Christ, joined with an apparent subjection to him, in embracing his gospel, and obeying his laws. Where there appears love to Jesus, and subjection to him as a Saviour, and a Sovereign, we are bound to consider such persons as related to him, and to love them accordingly. The apostle, treating of the visible church as in union with Christ, founded on profession, says, "We being many, are one body in Christ, and every one members one of another." Rom. xii. 5. And speaking of the churches of Judea, he adds, "which were *in* Christ." Gal. i. 22. To be, therefore, in the *church* by a credible profession, was called a being in *Christ*, as in 1 Cor. xii. 2. See Gal. iii. 27; 1 Cor. xii. 13.

It is evident that the apostle did not account all were true believers which were in Christ by profession, though he was bound in charity to hope thus of them all, till there was evidence to the contrary. The inspired penmen did not certainly know the gracious state of the persons they addressed, but had cheering hopes and distressing fears, respecting those to whom they ministered. See Epist. to Gal. Even Jesus, "who knew what was in man," generally, as a minister, addressed his own people by such terms as were descriptive of gracious dispositions. Matt. v.

As many are in Christ only by a profession, having a name to live, and are dead; therefore, there is a striking propriety in the various *ifs* we meet with in Scripture, when promises and encouragements are treated of, which *ifs* do not imply an uncertainty of a true believer's future happiness; but an uncertainty respecting who the persons are that have believed through grace. With what jealousy does Paul speak of the Galatian churches, and of many in that of Corinth; and with what caution does Peter mention one whom he greatly valued, "Sylvanus, a faithful brother, as I suppose." 2 Pet. v. 12. The visible kingdom of Christ is compared to a net which encloseth divers kinds: but the Lord, who searcheth the heart, will take care of the good, and cast the bad away. Then many who were visibly in connexion with Christ, who ate and drank in his presence, who were the children of the kingdom, and visible members of his body, the church, will be cast out; so hat those who are found fruitless branches in Christ, will be broken off, and burned with unquenchable fire. Therefore, it is granted that many who are in Christ, in this sense, i. e., *visibly*, may, notwithstanding, lift up their eyes in hell, being in torment.

Secondly. There is a *vital* union, or a divine connexion between Christ and his people, which takes place when the soul is made to hear the voice of the Son of God and live. Hence, the apostle says, "I live; yet not I, but Christ which liveth in me." To live implies three things, all which, in a spiritual sense, every true Christian is the subject of, viz.: SENSATION, ANIMATION, PRESERVATION.

1. SENSATION. They feel the burden of guilt, and are sensible of the plague of their own hearts. They are convinced of their wants and weakness, and are conscious of being in a condition both mean and miserable. They see their own deformity and Jehovah's beauty. Their ears are open to receive instruction; and the voice of God

in his word, whether terrific or tender, makes deep and durable impressions on their minds. They have a taste for the things of religion, after which they hunger and thirst. To them Christ is precious: his name is as ointment poured forth, his beauty is as the olive tree, and his smell as Lebanon; yea, he is "altogether lovely." All their spiritual sensations, whether painful or pleasurable, are in consequence, of living union with Jesus; for prior to its commencement they were dead in sin, and destitute of every holy emotion and perception.

2. Animation. Christian activity is entirely owing to Christ's animative influence. Through his Spirit and all-sufficient grace, they *serve* with pleasure, or *suffer* with patience; they war against sin, and wrestle with principalities and powers, over all which they are more than conquerors through him who hath loved them. Yea, they can do all things through Christ strengthening them, and without him they can do nothing.

3. Preservation. The principle of animation ever discovers an inclination to preserve its connexion with that which is animated by it: this is obvious not only in rational but in animal life. So, Christ has always discovered an entire, infinite inclination to keep and preserve his people in connexion with himself. He influences them to love,

and labor for the meat which perisheth not. He alarms their fears that they may escape danger, strengthens their faith that they may lay hold of eternal life, and secures their love by fresh discoveries of divine beauties, and the suitableness of celestial objects to heaven-born souls. Thus he draws them in the paths of duty by the bands of love, and by the cords of a man. He is the author of their preservation, in such a way as to prevent presumption, and secure their attention to appointed means, which Divine wisdom has connected with the desired end. He says he never will leave them, but will be with them always to the end of the world; and writes his law in their hearts, that they might not finally depart from him. He saves them, therefore, not contrary to their inclination, but with their free consent, and fervent desire. "He that is joined unto the Lord is one spirit." 1 Cor. vi. 17. Between Jesus and them, there is a oneness in *perception*, *affection*, *interest* and *end*. As they are precious to him, so he is precious to them; "the chiefest among ten thousand, and altogether lovely." His interest is theirs, and theirs is his. He rejoiceth in the prosperity of his people, and they esteem Jerusalem, (that is, his cause on earth,) above their chief joy. His revealed designs correspond with their real desires. The destruction of sin and the perfection of purity they long for. He gave his life for them, neither do they count theirs too dear to sacrifice on his behalf; their life, therefore, is in their hand, ready to be delivered up at their Saviour's call. They rejoice in Jesus on account of his mediatorial obedience, not only as it is their security from condemnation, but as it does infinite honor to Heaven's righteous law. What Christ has done, will intentionally and ultimately terminate in the vindication of God's moral government, and the eternal display of Jehovah's essential perfections, in all their infinite excellency, grandeur, and glory, that God, to whom sinners have an aversion, may appear and be acknowledged, not only by angels, but by men, as all in all. As influenced by grace, the true believer says, "Oh, how I love thy law!" "I delight in the law of God after the inward man." Jehovah he admires and adores; and when he takes a solemn view of the great Eternal, whose glory dazzles angelic eyes, he is astonished, confounded, and lost, in pleasing wonder. He sinks into profound contempt of himself, and feels keen reflections on his criminal departures from a Being so infinitely deserving the supreme love of men and angels. But on the revival of hope, with humble reverence, and holy rapture, he sings, "The Lord is my portion, saith my soul. He is my rock and fortress, and my deliverer, my God, my strength, my buckler, my salvation, and my high tower. In his presence is fulness of joy, at his right hand are pleasures for evermore. Then shall I be satisfied, when I awake in his likeness." Though conscious of meanness and demerit, his language now is, "Will he plead against me with his great power? No, but he will put strength into me." "I know whom I have believed. He hath said, My grace shall be sufficient for thee, my strength is made perfect in weakness. The Lord will preserve me unto his heavenly kingdom, to whom be glory for ever and ever. Amen."

As such souls freely give themselves unto the Lord, so he receives them graciously, and rejoiceth in them as his spouse, property, and portion; it is his will, and their desire to be like him, and with him forever; and for them to die is gain. Therefore, though mere professors perish, none who are possessors of his grace ever shall. Their internal life is eternal in its duration; for thus saith the Lord, "I give unto them eternal life; and they shall never perish, neither shall any pluck them out of my hand." John x. 28. "He that believeth on him is not condemned." John iii. 18. "There is therefore now no condemnation to them which are in Christ Jesus, who walk not after the flesh, but after the Spirit." Rom. viii. 1. As there is no condemnation to such now, there never shall be any. "Verily, verily, I say unto you, he that heareth my word and believeth on him that sent me, hath everlasting life, and shall not come into condemnation, but is passed from death unto life." John v. 24. "That whosoever believeth in him, should not perish, but have eternal life." John iii. 15, 16. "He that believeth in me, though he were dead, yet shall he live: and whosoever liveth and believeth in me, shall never die." John xi. 25, 26. "Who shall separate us from the love of Christ?" Rom. viii. 35. His Spirit is in them as "a well of water springing up into everlasting life." John iv. 14. "He that hath the Son hath life, and he that hath not the Son of God, hath not life." 1 John v. 12. Those, therefore, who are vitally united to Christ, cannot lose their spiritual life while he maintains his own; for he hath said, "Because I live, ye shall live also." Being bought by his precious blood, and kept by almighty power, they therefore may conclude with the apostle, that "when Christ, who is our life, shall appear, then shall ye also appear with him in glory." Col. iii. 4.

There is, therefore, no real contradiction in the declarations in Scripture, respecting the final state of those who are united to Christ; for salvation is not inseparably connected with a visible, but with a vital union to the Son of God. Those who perish never were spiritually in Christ: he was never the home of their hearts; they never approved of him, nor he of them; therefore he will say to all that shall be doomed to destruction, I never knew you. Though they may have been *among* the saints, yet such were never *of* them; but were of a contrary character all the while. Hence of apostates the apostle thus speaks: "They went out from us, but they were not of us; for if they had been of us, they would no doubt have continued with us: but they went out, that they might be made manifest, that they were not all of us. But ye have an unction from the Holy One." 1 John ii. 19, 20. Thus it appears that a visible and a vital union to Christ are very distinct; and yet they are not opposites, for a profession of Christ cannot be deemed contrary to a possession of him.

Thirdly. Vital union is distinct from *virtual*, though one is not contrary or opposite to the other. By virtual union with Christ, is intended a real connection subsisting between him and the elect of God considered simply as such.

That there was such a connexion antecedent to vital union, is evident from the following considerations. They were chosen in Christ, and given to him; in covenant he represented them as a federal head. He became a surety for them, and on their behalf was made under the law, in consequence of which there was a legal union established between him and them. The substitution of his person under the law in their stead, was the ground of the imputation of their sins to him, and of his obedience for them. What he did and endured, would have had no efficacy in their favor, had they not been personally interested in him. Their sins could not have been done away by the sacrifice of himself, had he not given himself for *them* in particular or died in their stead. But as their kinsman-Redeemer, he ransomed them from death, and as the Head of the church, he became the Saviour of the body.

Thus was he related to his chosen, as their head of representation; and, as their surety, by his gracious engagements and condescending substitution of his person to endure the penalties of the law in their place, and by his performing for them what was required of them, he became "the Lord their righteousness," and by his death he procured on their behalf an eternal exemption from deserved punishment, and a legal title to everlasting bliss. In consequence of this union, the elect were intrusted to his care, and were preserved in Christ Jesus, and, therefore, called to be saints. By virtue of the aforesaid connexion, they are said to be his sheep, whom he must bring; for of all that the Father hath given him, he will lose none:

and from thence ariseth the propriety of the apostle's language in Eph. ii. 4, 6: "God, who is rich in mercy, for his great love wherewith he loved us, even when we were dead in sins, hath quickened us together with Christ, and hath raised us up together, and made us sit together in heavenly places in Christ Jesus."

As this *virtual* union does not supersede *vital*, or render it unnecessary, but is the secret source from whence it flows, why then should the godly quarrel one with another about what is so evidently consistent? Though fruit be only found in the branches, yet the root is surely not unprofitable, seeing from thence the sap of the tree proceeds. According to this simile we may observe, what the Scripture calls "bringing forth fruit unto God," can only be expected among those professors of religion, who are in Christ as visible branches. But even amongst them, will no fruit be found without sap or living nourishment; and there can be no vital nourishment, but in consequence of union with the root. As none ever imagine there is no connexion between the root and branches of a tree till blossoms appear, why then should any think there is no connexion between Christ the root of the righteous, and his people, before the appearance of grace? It is owing to the appearance of gracious dispositions, that a relation to Christ is discovered, or claimable by any person: nevertheless, the union or relation in the last sense in which we have been speaking, does not then commence.

If there was no previous secret connexion with Christ, from whence did grace proceed to the soul? It must have a source or original cause. The apostle observes all spiritual blessings were given us in Christ. Eph. i. 3. If Christ was intrusted with all spiritual blessings to communicate to his people, then no spiritual blessing is ever possessed, but what flows from him; and if so, there must be a prior connexion with him. Believers have reason gratefully to acknowledge that "of his fulness have all we received, and grace for grace." John i. 16. To the hesitating soul we would recommend a close consideration of the apostle's query; "What hast thou that thou didst not receive?" 1 Cor. iv. 7.

The doctrine of union between Christ and his church is of a nature so copious, that no one metaphor can properly represent it; therefore in the Scriptures we meet with various similitudes, tending to illustrate the important subject. Christ is frequently compared to a *foundation*, on which his people are built; but that conveying only the idea of support, therefore he is compared to a *root*, by which the idea of influence is likewise illustrated. But though *branches* are influenced, and rendered fruitful, in consequence of conveyed nourishment, yet Christian activity is not thereby properly represented: to supply this defect, Christ and his people are farther illustrated by the union subsisting between *head* and *members*. But though the idea of activity is thereby conveyed, there is still a material defect, for the relation between these is quite *involuntary*. Had it been otherwise, the *head* might possibly have chosen better *feet*, or better *hands;* and had *they* been the subjects of distinct volition, they would, probably, have chosen to have been in union with a better *head:* therefore to supply the deficiency of the above simile, and to include the idea of *mutual* choice and social endearments, Christ and his church are compared to husband and wife.

If then we are in such near and close connexion with the blessed Jesus, as the Scriptures assert, and, by so many significant similitudes, illustrate his own people to be, let us frequently think of, and bless God for, that sovereign and inseparable love which constituted the relation.

CHAPTER V.

RELATION TO GOD.

LET us consider *on what,* relation to God is founded. That relation in which God's people stand unto himself, distinct from others, according to the Scripture, arises from adoption and regeneration. Adoption is the taking those into the relation of sons, and treating them as such, who are not so by nature. Now God's people were all by nature aliens; but, by adopting grace, they were by him considered as his children. Again, His people are all his children by birth; being born again, they partake of his nature, as it consists in righteousness and true holiness, and so bear his image. Adoption constitutes relation, but does not convey likeness of nature; but regeneration does both. Adoption is antecedent to regeneration, for there is no propriety in supposing those are made sons by adoption who are so by birth. No man ever adopted his own son; those who are sons by nature, need not to be made sons by adoption. Though the persons who are regenerated were adopted, yet they were not adopted as regenerate, but when they were in a state of alienation from God. In which state all men are by nature, as the descendants of an apostate head.

Adoption is, therefore, the taking of those into the relation of children, who are not so by nature, or accounting those sons, who are not, as yet, such by regeneration. Relation by adoption is, therefore, quite distinct from sonship arising from a being generated, and born anew; and accordingly we find it treated of as a separate subject in the word of God. Adoption is an act of God's sovereign *will.* "Having predestinated us unto the adoption of children by Jesus Christ to himself, according to the good pleasure of his will, to the praise of the glory of his grace, wherein he hath made us accepted in the Beloved." Eph. i. 5, 6. Regeneration is the work of his power, it is a manifest change of soul produced by his Holy Spirit. "Not by works of righteousness which we have done, but according to his mercy he saved us, by the washing of regeneration, and renewing of the Holy Ghost." Titus iii. 5.

The people of God, considered as children by adoption, were the subjects of redemption. Being, through sin, in a state of distance and dreadful captivity, Christ gave his life a ransom for them. "He died, the just for the unjust, that he might bring them to God." Those who were sometime afar off are made nigh by the blood of his Son. It was, therefore, expedient that Christ should die for the people, and gather together in one the children of God that were scattered abroad. John xi. 50, 52. "For it became him, for whom are all things, and by whom are all things, in bringing many sons unto glory, to make the captain of their salvation perfect through sufferings." Heb. ii. 10. They were not redeemed, considered as *saints*, but as *sinners;* not redeemed as children by regeneration, but as sons by adoption; and of them, as such, Christ will at the last say, "Father, here am I and the children which thou hast given me."

The application of redeeming love, and the possession of the Redeemer's purchase is not enjoyed, nor by them desired till renewed in the spirit of their minds; but being God's adopted sons, therefore, in his account they were entitled to them; and because they were sons, the Spirit of Christ is sent into their hearts, crying, Abba, Father. It is owing to the Spirit of adoption, or the Holy Ghost, bearing witness to their relationship as the children of God, that they are delivered from that bondage and fear which would otherwise overwhelm them, in consequence of a sight and sense of criminal distance from God, and unlikeness to him. Rom. viii. 15, 17.

The bodies of God's people were included in the act of adoption, and with their souls were given to Christ, and bought by him; "Ye are bought with a price, wherefore glorify God in your bodies,—which are his." But though the members of the body are instruments of righteousness unto holiness, in consequence of a person being renewed in the spirit of his mind, yet in this life the bodies of the saints have no peculiar marks of divine sonship, but are subject to vanity, bondage, and corruption. The privileges of adoption, therefore, as relating to them, will not be enjoyed till the resurrection, for the bodies of all men through sin are the seat of misery; and not only bodies in general, but ourselves also, which have the first fruits of the Spirit, "even we ourselves groan within ourselves, waiting for the adoption, to wit, the redemption of the body." Rom. viii. 23.

Sonship by adoption is not contrary to, nor does it render relationship to God by regeneration, unnecessary; there is as much need of a meetness for heaven as of a title to it. In order to consummate happiness, it is as necessary to have a disposition, or taste, for pure and refined pleasure, as it is to be delivered from pain. Therefore, except a man be born again, he cannot enter into the kingdom of God, he cannot see it in its nature, beauty, and spiritual glory, for the natural man perceiveth not the things of the Spirit of God, neither can he know them, because they are spiritually discerned. The doctrine of adoption is supporting to the believer's hope, even when he loathes and bemoans himself on the account of transgressions, for the very name Jesus (a Saviour) was given to Immanuel, because he should save *his* people from their sins. Matt. i. 21. But considered as born again, they are not denominated sinners, but saints, for he that is born of God sinneth not. Sin is not his occupation. By adoption God's people were in a point of relation made near to him, as respecting their persons; by regeneration they become followers of him as dear children, being the subjects of gracious principles and holy dispositions.

As sonship among men arises from adoption as well as from natural descent, the Lord, more fully to express his love to his people, and the ground of their title to heavenly things, has been pleased to discover himself as their Father under both considerations. This if properly attended to by the household of faith, their differences would in some measure subside, and their difficulties in some degree diminish; for according to the scriptural account of relation to God, they are most certainly right to say, that by regeneration or heavenly birth the people of God are denominated sons in a proper sense, and in which sense they were not his children before, for we are all the children of God by faith in Christ Jesus; and if any man have not the Spirit of Christ, he is none of his. But those who heartily subscribe to this truth, may, without offence, be allowed to say, that by adoption they were constituted sons *before* believing; for none are denominated believers till born of God, and it would be absurd to suppose they were not till then adopted. Equally absurd as to suppose Adam adopted Abel.

When the Scriptures treat *only* of men's relation to God, it is then attributed to adoption; or the gracious act of Jehovah's will towards them; which does not imply, but is distinct from, his powerful influences in and upon them; but when likeness and relation to God are jointly considered, a heavenly birth is then intended or included. The Holy Spirit's operations in the souls of men are illustrated by natural generation; because, such are thereby made partakers of the Divine image, as it consisteth in righteousness and true holiness. The consideration of these things, it is hoped, may tend to reconcile the minds of some of the people of God, and prevent their falling out by the way.

CHAPTER VI.

THE DOCTRINE OF ATONEMENT.

THIS important truth is attended with difficulties, which are perplexing to weak Christians, the removal of which calls for serious attention to its nature and necessity.

Atonement signifies reconciliation, or appeasing of anger. To atone is to harmonize or bring parties to an agreement that were at variance, so as to be *at one* again, or brought into a state of friendship, amity, and good will. The atonement under present consideration, is that by or on the account of which God is pacified towards, or pardons the sins of, his people. Various ideas are included in the term, as used in Scripture, but they are all of a kindred nature, and adhere to the important doctrine, as their central point, tending to explain its natural origin and efficacy. To obtain a distinct view of the subject, it may be proper to observe,

First. It supposes the party to whom satisfaction is due, has been justly injured or offended. This was the case in respect of God. Men are become enemies to him without any reason which can possibly exculpate them from blame. His law, which men have broken, is in every respect reasonable and right. His authority, though indisputably the highest and best founded, is treated by man with the greatest contempt. The moral beauty and excellency of God is disgustful to his rebellious creatures. As Jehovah is the first, the best, and most worthy of all beings, it is fit he should value and esteem his own glory in proportion to its worth, which is infinitely more excellent and more dear to him, than all creatures in heaven and earth. But man has set up his own honor and happiness in opposition to God's, and as it were deifies himself, and debases Jehovah, to whom he pays no further regard than he apprehends will terminate in his own advantage. God's anger is righteous displeasure, for men have hated him without a cause; there was nothing in his nature, character, or commands, with which men could be justly displeased. God never did any thing to provoke his creatures to revolt; if he had, he would have been under obligation to have made satisfaction to man for the injury done him, in order to an honorable reconciliation, that man might be just, and the justifier of God, which is shocking to suppose.

Secondly. The atonement supposes the offending party to have been justly deserving of punishment, and exposed to misery. If he was not exposed to misery, there could have been no need of mercy; and if he was the real offender, something was needful to atone for the offence, in order to a restoration of friendship between him and his Creator. There is a prevalent conviction attending guilt, of the necessity of something to recommend to and pacify offended Deity.

It is not against atonement that men are naturally prejudiced; but it is only that of God's providing, to which they have an aversion. "Wherewith shall I come before the Lord, and bow myself before the most high God?" is the common and grand inquiry of a guilty mind. God, through infinite wisdom and sovereign love, has made a gracious proclamation in favor of criminal man, saying, "Deliver his soul from going down to the pit, I have found a ransom," or an atonement. This was entirely a new procedure, the effect of a new and well-ordered covenant, according to his eternal purpose, which he purposed in Christ Jesus our Lord. There was nothing in God's law, nothing in the original constitution of things, nor any known property in Deity, from whence it could be inferred, that mercy would ever be shown to man, or friendship be restored between him and his justly offended Sovereign. The gracious intention was *hid* in God. Eph. iii. 9.

Yea, had an intimation been given of the kind design, the nature of atonement is such that created wisdom could never have guessed *how*, or by whom it could be accomplished. For,

1. The person undertaking to atone, must have been able to offer to God that which was infinite in its worth and value.

2. He must have the *nature* of those whom his atonement is to benefit; i. e. he must be MAN, capable of obeying the law, and bearing its tremendous curse, without personal and perpetual destruction.

3. He who atones for another's crimes must himself be innocent, otherwise an atonement would be needful on his own account; and therefore, whatever he might do or endure for the purpose of reconciliation, could not benefit any other guilty person. But among men, where could perfect innocence be found, seeing the whole world is become guilty before God? But supposing such a one could have been found, an atonement would not have appeared possible, because,

4. Equity cannot allow an innocent person to suffer punishment. It is contrary to the natural rule of right; penal suffering cannot be inflicted but in consequence of guilt: therefore he that justifieth the wicked, and he that condemneth the just, even they both are an abomination to the Lord. Prov. xvii. 15. And shall not the Judge of all the earth

do right? It is not possible he should do that which is abhorrent to his nature, and abominable in his sight; therefore, as a God of equity he cannot clear the guilty, nor punish the innocent.

5. He who is supposed to endure vicarious punishment, or suffer in the room and stead of another, must stand in such prior relation to or union with him, on whose behalf he is punished, as is necessary to support the delinquent's claim to an equitable discharge. But where could such a friend be found, standing judicially related to miserable man, to act as his surety, or as a day's man, between him and his God, and lay his hand upon them both? Job ix. 33; xvii. 3. But on a supposition that such a friend could have been pointed out, who was allowedly one in law with the sinner, yet he could not die, or suffer in his stead, though even desirous of it, because,

6. No *creature* has power or authority over his own life, to lay it down when he pleases, nor even to suffer mutilation on behalf of his dearest friend; for his life and his limbs are at the sole and only disposal of God.

From the above, and similar considerations, it appears, that the nature of sin, and the condition of men, were such as totally to preclude every ray of hope, yea, every idea of the possibility of an atonement being made, or a reconciliation accomplished.

But in the glorious gospel, God has opened a door of hope for lost sinners. He has graciously provided and revealed a method of salvation, a contrivance wherein he hath abounded towards us in all wisdom and prudence. Eph. i. 8. For every difficulty vanishes when the glorious Immanuel is viewed as the atoning priest and bleeding victim.* Here is infinite worth, value and virtue,

* Let us examine the preceding numbered paragraphs in the light of Scripture; and we shall perhaps see more fully what was the meaning of our author, and what is Scripture truth on the subject. He says,

1. "He who would atone must offer what is of infinite value." The blood of bulls and lambs cannot atone, therefore he says "Lo I COME." Why? that he might do what they could not:—"he taketh away the first to establish the second." He came to "take away sin by the sacrifice of himself." See Heb. x. 4—10; ix. 26.

2. "He must be man." And accordingly "He took on him the seed of Abraham." "The word was made flesh." And we read, "He was raised for our justification" after being "delivered for our offences," i. e. his resurrection evinced that his sacrifice was sufficient and accepted, and that justice had no further claims; and hence "Christ being raised, dieth no more; death hath no more dominion over him," and we are "begotten again to a lively hope of an incorruptible inheritance by his resurrection from the dead." See Heb. ii. 16; John i. 14; Rom iv. 25; vi. 9; 1 Pet. i. 3.

"He must be innocent." His blood was as that "of a lamb without blemish and without spot." He was just such a High Priest as our case required—"holy, harmless, undefiled, separate from sinners." Hence "he needed not," as Levitical

infinite ability to obey the precepts of the law, and endure its awful penalty, without sustaining the loss of final felicity. He was holy, harmless and separate from sinners. But that he might legally suffer, the just for the unjust, he who knew no sin was made sin for us. The Lord laid on him the iniquity of us all, which he bore in his own body on the tree, when he made his soul an offering for sin. Thus, through imputation, he was numbered with transgressors, and bore the sins of many,

---

priests, "to offer daily, for his own sins." 1 Pet. i. 19; Heb. vii. 26, 27.

4. "It is inequitable that an innocent person should suffer punishment;" and it was not, strictly speaking, *punishment* which Jesus did endure. "But it *became* him by whom and for whom are all things, to make the Captain of our salvation perfect through *sufferings*," and this was done without iniquity, "for he *gave* his life a ransom." It was not "*taken* from him; but he laid it down of *himself;* and had a right to do so; being himself "the Prince of life." See above under 6. Heb. ii. 10; Matt. xx. 28; John v. 26.

5. "To render equitable the delinquent's discharge, he who suffers vicariously must have previously sustained a relation to him." Such a relation existed, and was recognised: "As for thee also by the blood of THY COVENANT I have sent forth THY PRISONERS out of the pit wherein is no water." Zech. ix. 11.

6. "No creature has power or authority over his own life, &c." But the Messiah is not a creature: he is "over all, God blessed for ever." "The second man is THE LORD from heaven." Rom. ix. 5; 1 Cor. xv. 47. J. A. W.

which he put away by the sacrifice of himself. What he did and endured in the room and stead of his people, was righteously placed to their account; he being graciously substituted in their stead, being their surety, made under the law, that he might redeem them from the curse of the law, being made a curse for them. He, therefore, kindly gave his life a ransom for his people, for he had authority and power to lay down his life, and power to take it up again. This commandment, says he, I received of my Father. His propitiatory death was according to the determinate counsel and foreknowledge of God, and agreeable to the everlasting covenant, and therefore with his full approbation and free consent.

Christ's atonement was illustrated by the various atonements under the law, and was the central point of them. The respective victims were without blemish; were the property of the persons on whose account they were to be offered; the crimes they were designed to expiate were first solemnly confessed over them, and then as having sin transferred to them, they were offered up as the sinner's substitute, in consequence of which temporary forgiveness was obtained; for these were only shadows of good things to come, and were offered year by year continually, but could never make the comers thereunto perfect, or take away sin as pertaining to the conscience. The law could make nothing perfect, but the bringing in of a better hope did. See Hebrews x. *Atonement* is a declaration of divine righteousness, and a vindication of Jehovah's justice in condemning and punishing for sin; therefore the act of Phineas, in taking vengeance in behalf of God on daring offenders, is called an atonement for the congregation. Atonement is designed as a covering of the guilty soul; whereby their iniquities are covered, and their transgressions are forgiven. When the congregation was numbered, it was enjoined on every man to give to the Lord a ransom for his soul; the rich were not to give more than half a shekel,* nor the poor less; which was called atonement money, as thereby atonement was made for their souls. In consequence of which price, they were covered from the plague to which they were liable. See Exodus xxx. 12, 16. So Jesus gave himself a ransom for many: his people were bought with a price, not with silver or gold, but with the precious blood of the Son of God, in whom we have redemption, even the forgiveness of sins. By the blessed Jesus, the purity of God's law was fully approved and eternally preserved, its righteous claims established and fully confirmed;

* A little over twenty-five cents, and so within the compass of the poor.

its tremendous curse was by him endured, and his people exempted from wrath to come. In him mercy and truth are met together, righteousness and peace have kissed each other. He is the true antitype of the mercy-seat, whom God hath sent forth to be a propitiation through faith in his blood. The seat of mercy where Deity appeared propitious, was the cover of, and supported by the ark, which contained and preserved the holy law which men had violated, denoting that the glory of God's righteous government must be secured before pardoning mercy could be discovered.

To deny the glory and equity of God's law, by which sinners are condemned, antecedent to the gospel, is to undermine the foundation of mercy, and destroy the pillars which support the throne of rich, reigning grace. The blood of atonement, sprinkled annually on the mercy-seat by the high priest, was an acknowledgment of Israel's guilt, and Jehovah's just authority; and likewise of their absolute dependence on his voluntary mercy, richly dispensed and gloriously displayed, consistent with his infinite hatred to sin and inflexible regard to impartial justice and punitive equity.

Some represent the atonement of Christ as unnecessary in order to the pardon of sin, the remission of which is, by them, considered as an act of divine clemency, without respect had to any merit attending the sufferings of Christ in the stead of those whose transgressions are forgiven. By this many have been perplexed, seeing such a view of things evidently tends to lessen the odious nature of sin, tarnish the lustre of Jehovah's character, and diminish the believer's obligation to Jesus. We therefore shall consider,

1. It is undeniable that a consciousness of sin is attended with a fear of punishment in those who are not favored with a divine revelation. Hence the apostle, speaking of the heathen world, says, "Who knowing the judgment of God, that they which commit such things are worthy of death." Rom. i. 32. If punishment be not necessarily connected with transgression, how could the dread of suffering, and a conviction of the righteousness of God in taking vengeance, be so deeply engraven on the hearts of those who did not know the will and determination of God, except as inferred from the natural obligation his creatures are under to glorify him as their Creator.

No creature can possibly know what originates in the sovereign will of God, without a divine revelation; but as the punishment of sin can be known where a revelation is not possessed, therefore the punishment of sin arises not from divine sovereignty, but from the essential purity, dignity, and rectitude of Jehovah's nature; and hence there was a necessity for Christ, as the surety, to endure the penalty, in order to his people's enjoying a pardon; for sin is so abominable in God's sight, so contrary to his pure nature, that punishment for it cannot be dispensed with; a sinner, as such, cannot be safe. Hence, there was a necessity for Jesus the Saviour to put away sin, by the sacrifice of himself, to endure the curse, that his people might be exempted from sin's demerit, enjoy heavenly blessings, and wear the celestial crown.

2. Through the sufferings of Christ the essential righteousness of God is discovered, and his equity in acquitting the believer is thereby evidenced, and on that basis eternally established.

It is Jesus Christ, as a Redeemer, "Whom God hath sent forth to be a propitiation through faith in his blood, to declare his righteousness for the remission of sins that are past," (i. e., the sins of the Old Testament saints,) "through the forbearance of God: to declare, I say, at this time, his righteousness, that he might be just and the justifier of him that believeth in Jesus." Rom. iii. 25, 26. If God could with equity have pardoned sin, and justified criminals by an act of sovereign clemency, without an atonement, the death of Jesus did *not* render the sinner's acquittal just and righteous, as the apostle asserts. But as the equity of God in justifying the ungodly, depends upon the Saviour's sufferings, therefore, without his sufferings there could have been no pardon of sin granted; for "all his ways are judgment, a God of truth, and without iniquity, just and right is he." Deut. xxxii. 4.

When we say, God could not pardon sin without an atonement, or that "without shedding of blood there is no remission," a limitation of Jehovah's power is not intended, nor is it from thence inferable; for pardon and justification are not productions of Divine power, but of his will. Besides, God cannot do what is improper. He cannot lie, he cannot deny himself; and of iniquity he says, "I cannot away with it;" not owing to a deficiency in power, but the perfection of his purity, and rectitude of his nature.

3. God's gift of his Son to die for us, is always, in Scripture, admired as the greatest and most astonishing instance of his love to sinners, and considered as a blessing superior to any other conferred on his people. Hence, the apostle infers, "if God spared not his own Son, but delivered him up for us all, how shall he not, with him, freely give us all things?" Rom. viii. 32. But if sinners could have been made happy without Jesus, if there was no real necessity for his death, the gift of Christ, by such an awful supposition,

is diminished in value, and the favor sinks into the number of non-essentials in point of eternal felicity.

4. If Divine justice could have dispensed with the punishment of sin, Christ was so precious to his righteous Father, and so entirely loved by him, that it is natural to suppose he would have been spared; those agonizing sorrows and excruciating pains, under which he groaned and died, would not have been, without necessity, inflicted upon the darling of heaven. But as sin was placed to his account, it pleased the Father to bruise him, and put him to grief; though he pleaded to have the cup removed, if possible, yet he spared him not.

Now as in every other thing the Father heard him always, may we not from thence conclude, it was impossible for the connexion between *sin* and *suffering* to be broken? Who can attend to the tremendous language of a sin-avenging God, saying, "Awake, O sword, against the man that is my fellow," smite him; or seriously reflect on the doleful groans and bloody sufferings of the Son of God, in the garden, and on the cross; and calmly conclude there was no necessity for any thing of that nature.

5. Those who are redeemed from sin, and reign with God in heavenly pomp and holy splendor, ascribe their deliverance and advancement to the

kindness of Christ, and the efficacy of his sufferings; for with triumphant pleasure and gratitude they sing, "Unto him that loved us, and washed us from our sins in his own blood, and hath made us kings and priests unto God and his Father, to him be glory and dominion for ever and ever. Amen." Rev. i. 5, 6. But how does the propriety of such acknowledgments appear, if what Jesus did was not at all necessary to their deliverance from sin and advancement to dignity and delight? From the above considerations it appears, there was a necessity for Jesus to die, the just for the unjust, that he might bring them to God.

Some admit the death of Christ to be necessary, in order to the forgiveness of sins, yet deny him the honor of properly meriting for his people an exemption from punishment, and *assert that the efficacy of his sufferings as a sacrifice arose entirely from the will and appointment* of God.* That

---

* This opinion is sometimes advanced by persons who are the farthest possible from desiring to detract from the glory of the Redeemer. Let such persons carefully weigh the reasoning of this author, and they will see cause to relinquish their opinion. In confirmation of his position the following considerations are offered to the reader.

1. Sin cannot be forgiven without a satisfaction to eternal justice. Justice is an essential attribute of Deity; if its claims are compromised, the basis of Divine government is under-

he became a mediator, surety, and sacrifice on behalf of his people, in consequence of Divine ap-

---

mined: for "justice and judgment are the establishment(see margin) of his throne." Sin has merited punishment; its wages is death. The blood of bulls and goats cannot take away sin; and yet it *must* be removed, and blood (i. e., death) is requisite to remove it. Heb. ix. 22. "The Lamb of God really taketh away the sin of the world," and Christ is that Lamb. Hence, the death of Christ is a REAL sacrifice; i. e., it takes away sin in virtue of its inherent efficacy; and not merely because it was appointed to do so. "He is the propitiation for our sins."

2. The Prophets taught the reality of his sacrifice. What other interpretation can be put on such passages as the following? Isa. liii. 4—6, 8, 10, 11, 12, and Dan. ix. 24. 26. Here is nothing indicative of the efficacy of his sufferings being derived from his being appointed; but on the contrary, the clearest statements that his sufferings were substitutionary, and his sacrifice real. True, he was "set forth as a propitiation;" but his being set forth did not render him such. He was set forth as such, because he *was* such, and as the apostle says, for these two purposes: First, "that God might *be* just" in forgiving sin; and Secondly, that he might *appear* just:—"to *declare* his righteousness in the forgiveness of sins that are past," and "that God might be just and the justifier of him that believeth." Neither of these purposes could have been accomplished if justice had not been satisfied: unless (which will not be supposed) God should sacrifice his truth by appearing just, when in fact he was not so. But if justice be satisfied with the death of Jesus, our position is established; and the death of Christ was a REAL sacrifice.

3. The New Testament writers are explicit to the same point. 2 Cor. v. 21: "He made him to be a sin-offering for us." Gal. iii. 13: "Christ hath redeemed us from the curse,—

pointment, is undoubtedly evident; but that his *value* and worth, efficacy, and merit, arose from thence, can never be proved. God graciously provided the ransom, on which account pardon, justification, and the whole of salvation is all of free, exuberant grace, and mercy. That a person of such infinite worth and dignity as Immanuel, God's own, and only begotten Son, should die for sinners, is an unparalleled instance of favor and love. It is the wonder of angels, the terror of devils, and the joy and triumph of saints.

But it is absurd to suppose his personal dignity to arise from his debasement, that he became strong, because help was laid upon him, or that his real worth arose from his appointment to ransom miserable captives, and discharge the debt of prodigal transgressors. Christ was appointed, and agreed in covenant to do and suffer what he was under no natural obligation to perform or endure; and

---

being made a curse for us." 1 Pet. ii. 24: "Who his own self bare our sins in his own body on the tree."—iii. 18: "Christ suffered for sins, the just for the unjust."

The obvious meaning of these passages is, that Jesus endured all that justice required, instead of those in whose place he stood; and thus secured, for them, exemption from its endurance. If he endured less than this, justice is not satisfied, and the Divine honor is tarnished. If he endured this, his death was, as we have seen above, a REAL sacrifice.

J. A. W.

from his native dignity, worth, and ability, arose his merit and efficacy. To suppose God appointed his death to be efficacious without real efficacy, or meritorious without personal merit, is a contradiction in terms, an awful reflection on the Divine understanding, and an affront to common sense.

Again, if God accepted of the death of Jesus as meritorious, though it was not so in its own nature, then might he have pardoned sins by a simple act of sovereign clemency, without the death of his Son; for it would surely have been equally just to have pardoned sin without a sacrifice, as to remit sin in consequence of that which is, in its nature, destitute of merit and efficacy.

Once more, if merit and real efficacy arise only from the Divine appointment, it would have been possible for the blood of bulls and of goats, or any other animal, to have taken away sin, if God had been pleased to have appointed such an end to have been answered by their death. But the direct contrary is asserted. "For it is not possible that the blood of bulls and of goats should take away sins;" Heb. x. 4; "which sacrifices can never take away sins;" verse 11. It was necessary that the patterns of things in the heavens should be purified with these, but the heavenly things themselves with better sacrifices than these. But now once in the end of the world hath he

(Christ) appeared, to put away sin by the sacrifice of himself." Heb. ix. 23, 26. He has "made peace by the blood of his cross, Col. i. 20, "having obtained eternal redemption for us," Heb. ix. 12, "to make an end of sin, and to make reconciliation for iniquity, and to bring in everlasting righteousness, Dan. ix. 24, with which "the Lord is well pleased," Isaiah xlii. 21. Therefore to every believer Jehovah says, "Fury is not in me." Isaiah xxvii. 4.

It is hoped that the above remarks may help the Christian over the objections made against the necessity, merit, and efficacy of the Saviour's death, as an atoning sacrifice, and tend to increase his knowledge of, faith in, and love to the blessed Jesus, as able to save to the uttermost all that come unto God by him. I should therefore add no more on the subject, were it not for another stumbling-block lately thrown in the way of believers, equally, if not more formidable in appearance than the above: which is,

If Christ was a Divine person, he could not atone for sin, because Deity could not die.

This objection seems intended to draw the unwary Christian into a dreadful dilemma, either to give up the soul-supporting doctrine of the atonement, or to deny the divinity of the Son of God. The objection is the more dangerous, as it seems to look on the doctrine of the atonement with a smiling countenance. But, in fact, the design of it is to undermine the real personal merit of Christ, and place the efficacy of his blood to the account of God's appointment, as mentioned above. The disguised intention of the objection is this: "Sinners, you must be content with a finite creature Saviour, or none at all. If Christ be God, he is too great to do you any essential service as a Saviour, because Deity cannot die. Therefore do not think sin is infinitely odious and hateful to God. It does not merit infinite displeasure and punishment. If it did, there could be no infinite satisfaction made to God; for even supposing Christ to be Divine, his sacrifice could not be of infinite value, because as a Divine person he could not die." Let us calmly consider this objection, and seriously attend to the supposed dreadful dilemma, in which will be found more sophistry than sense.

Death always implies a loss of that wherein life consisted. Death, in the sense we are now called to consider it, is a separation of the principle of sensation and influence; thus it is said, "The body without the spirit is dead." Without the soul it is in a state of total inactivity, incapable of voluntary motion, and divested of sensation. Now though the body only be the subject of death, considered as a state of inactivity and insensibility, yet the man is said to be dead, when soul and body, the constituent parts of humanity, are separated, although the soul or spirit, distinctly considered from the body, is not the subject of death. A spirit cannot die, because it is of a simple or uncompounded nature. There is no part of a soul, from whence another part can be divided. If a soul can be so separated, consciousness either does, or does not, continue in each separate part. If each part remain conscious, then are they two souls, or conscious subsistences. If one separated part of the soul remain unconscious, or in a state of insensibility, wherein does that part differ from matter?

A created spirit might cease to exist, if God so determined; but die it cannot. Annihilation is not death. What is annihilated has no existence, but what is dead *exists,* however its form be changed. There is therefore no force in the objection, Deity cannot die; for as no *spirit* can die, it might as pertinently be objected, if Christ had a soul he could not atone for sin, because a soul cannot die. The death of a spirit cannot be supposed; yet a man being composed of body and spirit, is with propriety said to be dead, when matter and mind, those constituent parts of humanity, are separated. Dead saints are therefore said to "rest in their beds," in respect of their bodies: yet in reference to their souls, "each one is walking in his uprightness." Death is therefore called a departure. "The time of my departure is at hand." Now as the Divine and human Spirit of our Immanuel ceased to animate his body, the person of the Mediator may as properly be said to have been dead, as the person of Samuel, David, or any other.

It may be necessary to observe, that death does not dissolve the *relation* between the body and spirit, but death consists in a cessation of vital influence, or a removal from the body, for a period, of the principle of sensation and animation. But the relative union still continuing, therefore the spirits of martyrs are represented as concerned about, and longing for their bodies, which were killed for the cause of Christ on earth, and at the resurrection every soul will have its own body. As through the separation of body and soul, and the relation between them being undissolved, the *man* is properly dead, and yet the soul not changed in its natural powers; so, in like manner, and for the same reason, it appears the person of the Mediator was really dead for a time, his precious body not being *animated* by, though related to, his human and Divine spirit. Yet his death does not imply the least change or mutability in its Divine nature, nor any alteration in the properties of his soul.

Agreeably to the above view of things we are told, that when the beloved disciple saw his Lord in transcendent splendour and glory, and fell at his feet as dead, the reviving and compassionate language of Jesus was, "Fear not, I am the first and the last: I am he that liveth and was dead; and behold, I am alive for evermore, Amen; and have the keys of hell and of death." Rev. i. 17, 18. That he, the first and the last, was dead, is again repeated in the solemn message sent to the church at Smyrna. Rev. ii. 8. Thus there is no force in the objection aforesaid; for instead of Christ's divinity rendering him incapable of atoning for sin, the infinite value attending the sufferings of his humanity arose from its union with the Divine nature, as one person. By virtue of which union his blood is divinely precious, and called the blood of God: like as the spirits under the altar called the blood with which they sealed their testimony for God, when in the body, *our blood.*

There is a value attending simple matter, considered as the production of God, who made every thing very good; yet animated matter is superior to what is not so, though it were an inferior form; otherwise a living dog would not be better than a dead lion, nor the body of a man preferable to a bag of sand. Animated bodies rise in value and respect, in proportion to the natural superiority of the spirits by which they are governed; though the body of a sparrow is the subject of animation as much as the body of a man, yet a human body is of more value than many sparrows. Again, the importance of actions through the medium of matter arises from the volitions and influence of the spirit by which they are performed; were it not so, the action of a man would not excel those of a monkey. Moreover, in regard to human nature, there is a great disproportion in real worth, arising from internal qualities, or external dignity; for scarcely for a righteous man will one die, yet peradventure for a good man, some would even dare to die. Hence David's adherents said, "Thou art worth ten thousand of us." How infinitely precious and worthy then was the Divine Jesus, in whom dwelt all the fulness of the Godhead bodily. May every believer's heart glow with love and gratitude for him, and say, with unfeigned lips, "Thanks be to God for his unspeakable gift."

PART II.

EXPERIMENTAL DIFFICULTIES.

CHAPTER I.

A SINNER'S WARRANT TO APPLY TO CHRIST.

It is common for those who are convinced of sin, and see the need of salvation, to look for some good thing in themselves, as the ground of encouragement for their applying to and closing with the blessed Jesus. But finding themselves altogether vile, sinful, and unworthy, they apprehend it would be daring presumption, in their present condition, to trust in, or apply to him for salvation. The stumbling-block, in this case, seems to arise from a mistaken apprehension,* accounting that which

* There is another misapprehension, the correction of which may relieve the perplexity of the persons in question. They confound Christ, the Messiah, with simple Deity; and as God "cannot look on iniquity with allowance, they draw the same conclusions respecting Christ. But Christ, though *truly* God, is not *merely* God. To God the sinner needs a *medium* of approach;—not so to Christ, who is, in one person, God and

supports a person's right to come to Christ as synonymous with, or equivalent to, what evidences an interest in him; or, in other words, persons want to know that they are really converted before they dare apply to Jesus. What greatly tends to entangle and retard the progress of such souls, are certain injudicious and dangerous maxims relating to *experimental religion.*

First. Some suggest, that it is not the duty of unconverted people to pray. Now if so, in order to a conviction of prayer being a duty, the prayerless person, even while continuing so, must have evidence of a conversion to God, which is absurd. Though Peter perceived that Simon the sorcerer was in the gall of bitterness and in the bond of iniquity, yet he directed him to penitence and prayer. It is evident there can be no gracious acts, but in consequence of gracious principles; yet it is equally evident, that gracious principles

---

man. To him the sinner may approach *as a sinner.* To the Father, no man can approach but by Christ; but to Christ the sinner may come immediately. True, Christ infinitely hates sin, and hates it in the applicant; but he is the friend of the sinner, and to him the sinner may come confidently. And *every* sinner may do so; for the warrant of an approach to him is not any merit in the applicant, nor any knowledge of the divine purpose to accept him in particular; but it is the invitation given to *all,* and a knowledge from divine declarations, of a purpose to receive ALL WHO APPLY. J. A. W.

cannot be discerned but by gracious acts; therefore such acts must necessarily precede, or be prior to the discernment of spiritual principle. It is therefore impossible for any man to know or to feel himself to be the subject of grace while he is prayerless, or to have the least evidence of his relation to Christ, without a reliance upon him and delight in him.

To assert, therefore, that persons are not to pray till they are converted, is dangerous and absurd. Dangerous, as it leads to a state of deception, and is the very essence of pharisaism; for such as think themselves converted before they come to Christ, by penitential prayer and faith, found their hopes on self-righteousness: the secret language of their deceived hearts is, "God be thanked I am not like other men," stand by, thou unconverted sinner, I am holier than thou. Such do not go to Chirst as a trembling criminal, but a confident convert; not as an undone sinner, but a self-admired saint. And such a representation is dangerous, as it tends to keep a carnal mind in profound and fatal peace; for such a man lives without prayer, and consequently without God, yet his conscience does not, cannot accuse him with the neglect of duty. If he ought not to pray, an aversion to prayer is not criminal, but commendable; for surely a person is to be commended for being averse to what he ought not to do. If it be said, that unregenerate men ought not to pray, because while in such a state they are incapable of spiritual actions, such objectors ought to point out what duties the unconverted can perform acceptably, or allow that they are not bound to the performance of any. And if not under obligation to obedience, they are not chargeable with sin, and consequently are not exposed to punishment; for whoever are not culpable, need not fear the Divine displeasure. But God has said he will pour out his fury on all them who call not on his name.

It is shocking to think that any poor sinner should be taught to consider himself exempted from an acknowledgment to God for the mercies he enjoys, and likewise from an application to him for present or future favors. Besides, it is absurd to assert, that a person ought not to pray until he feels himself converted, for it is much the same as saying a man ought not to ask for guidance until he knows he is right, nor seek for a cure till he feels himself healed.

Second. Another stumbling maxim is, No man can be the subject of genuine repentance till he he beholds by faith the Redeemer as dying for his transgressions, or at least have hope that his sins are forgiven him. A poor wounded sinner, not being so favored, is thereby taught to consider the way to the Saviour as barred against him; yea to conclude it would be an affront to the Lord for him to pray, "take away all iniquity;" or so much as to cry, "God be merciful to me a sinner!"

But is it not strange that a person cannot be sorry for a fault till he hopes he shall not be punished; nor sincerely beg for a favor till he enjoys it? How shall a person while he is in a state of impenitency, know that Christ died for him in particular? There is nothing in Scripture to encourage an impenitent sinner to believe that he is in a safe condition, but the very reverse is plainly and awfully expressed, "Thou,—after thy hardness and impenitent heart, treasurest up unto thyself wrath against the day of wrath and revelation of the righteous judgment of God." Rom. ii. 5. "For except ye repent, ye shall all likewise perish." Luke xiii. 3. "If we confess our sins, God is faithful and just to forgive us our sins;" but the sense of no Scripture is, if God will give us assurance, or hope of a pardon, we will be faithful and just to acknowledge our offences.

If there be no true repentance till the soul behold by faith the Redeemer as dying for its sins, then are we presented with a strange view of an impenitent believer, one who believes his sins are pardoned, for the commission of which he was never sorry! The Scriptures represent the nature of repentance and faith, and the connexion between them, as the very reverse of these raw and rash assertions. "Repent and be converted, that your sins may be blotted out when the times of refreshing shall come from the presence of the Lord." Acts iii. 19. Repentance towards God and faith towards our Lord Jesus Christ are subjects so important and comprehensive, as to include the substance of the great apostle's ministry: the necessity of repentance in order to the hope of pardon through faith in the blood of Jesus, he constantly testified both to Jews and Greeks. Acts xx. 21.

Christ is exalted to give first repentance; and *then* remission of sins to Israel. Acts v. 31. Pardon of sin is never, in all the Scripture, declared as belonging to the impenitent, but its uniform language is agreeable to the solemn assertion of the Son of God;. "Except ye repent, ye shall all likewise perish." Luke xiii. 3. 5. Therefore, the belief of a pardon is not prior to repentance; for repentance, indeed, implies knowledge of, and belief in the righteous and holy nature of God and his law, and a persuasion of personal criminality, as represented in the word of God. It consists in a pungent sense of the evil of sin;—a loathing and hearty forsaking of it; and humiliation for it; joined with a justification of the righteousness of God in passing sentence on the guilty criminal.

Repentance, therefore, implies the primary actings of faith, and is the immediate effect of grace in the soul; but the first actings of faith are not a believing the person is pardoned. Nothing can be more false than that an impenitent person has a revealed right to pardon; if he ought to believe he is pardoned before he repents, then he ought to believe a lie. But the most firm, hearty, and constant belief of a falsehood will never make it a truth. To suppose a person to believe in Christ as a dying Saviour, without repentance, is the same as supposing a man to need a physician, and long for a cure, while he is whole. But that such need not a physician, but they that are sick; see Matt. ix. 12.

It is impossible that a faith can be right, which springs from an impenitent heart, and which consists in believing that to be a fact, of the truth of which there is no evidence. If such a faith be not genuine, how can a false faith produce true repentance? Repentance is proved to be of a genuine spiritual nature, by its continuance and increase, when the fault repented of is remitted. But the conviction of blame does not spring from a forgiveness of the crime. Legal repentance, or the terrific operation of the law on the conscience without the grace of the gospel, arises from the sense of danger, and is continued and increased only by the fear of punishment; therefore, when danger disappears, and self is supposed to be safe, such a repentance immediately dies, the idea of danger being its sole support. But true repentance arising from a change of heart, a new and holy principle, and consisting in an aversion to sin, considered in its *power* and *pollution*, as well as its *punishment*, therefore, a sense of pardon, though it does not give existence or being to repentance, greatly increases a godly sorrow for sin, the evil of which is more deeply impressed on the mind from a view of the Saviour's sufferings, and the infinitely amiable character of God as a righteous lawgiver and loving Father.

Such a view melts the soul into evangelical sorrow for sin, and inflames the mind with indignation against it, and a vehement desire after its total destruction; called by the apostle *revenge*. 2 Cor vii. 11. When God pours on his chosen the spirit of grace, he first convinceth the soul of sin, and is then to his people a Spirit of supplication; and such suppliants, saith the Lord, shall look upon him whom they have pierced, and they shall mourn as one mourneth for his only son. Zech. xii. 10. The language of the true penitent, under the enjoyment of a full pardon, is beautifully set forth in the following lines of Watts:

> Whilst, with a melting, broken heart,
> My murdered Lord I view,
> I'll raise revenge against my sins,
> And slay the murderers too.

Third. It is frequently asserted, that a true faith in Christ is inseparably connected with the knowledge of an interest in him, or that there can be no proper believing in Jesus without considering him as a person's own. This has proved a stumbling block to many; for as common sense suggests the absolute necessity of evidence, in order to support a claim, and the soul before it goes to Christ not having that evidence, it therefore is discouraged from applying to him, till *proof* of an interest in him appear. Laboring in vain for marks and signs, as evidences of their belonging to Christ, in order to warrant or encourage their application to him, they conclude there is no hope, they are none of his chosen and redeemed, &c.

But there is no doctrine contained in the gospel, nor even any threatening in the law of God, which is a bar to an undone sinner's coming to Christ for salvation. Their right to come to Christ, does not in the least depend upon, or arise from, a prior knowledge of interest in special blessings, or feeling themselves the subjects of supernatural principles. Such experience, is obtained only in consequence of believing in or receiving Jesus the Saviour; for he who believeth not, is declared to be under condemnation;—the wrath of God abideth on him. To attempt, therefore, to define as some do, who ought, and who ought not to return to God by Christ, is daring presumption, and tends to discourage the soul, and rivet the fetters of guilt, where a sense of meanness and misery prevails, and in others, to encourage self-righteousness, by establishing the idea of previous fitness in order to salvation.

If any one should ask, Have I a right to apply to Jesus the Saviour, simply as a poor, undone, perishing sinner, in whom there appears no good thing? I answer, Yes; the gospel proclamation is, "Whosoever will, let him take the water of life freely." Rev. xxii. 17. "Unto you, O men, I call; and my voice is to the sons of man." Prov. viii. 4. The way to Jesus is graciously laid open for every one who chooses to come to him. His arms of mercy are expanded to receive the coming soul. Fear not, poor sinner, to approach him, he will not, on any account, cast thee out. John vi. 37. He does not receive with reluctance; no, it is his joy, it is his delight to save to the uttermost all that come unto God by him.

His endearing invitations to poor heavy-laden sinners, his melting expostulations with them, and gracious reception of them, are left on record as the warrant, and for the encouragement of sinners; therefore, the worst of such, even the vilest of the vile, may come to him for salvation. However remote you are, however great the distance from him, he kindly invites you to view him as the almighty Saviour; saying, "Behold me; Behold me!" Isaiah lxv. 1. "Look unto me, and be ye saved, all ye ends of the earth; for I am God, and there is none else." Isaiah xlv. 22. The gracious grant is indefinite;—the way to Jesus is open and free to *whosoever will*, without exception; nothing that God has done or said, is an obstacle.

To infer that personal unworthiness, or any scriptural doctrine, is a bar in the way to Jesus, is either the effect of strong temptations, or owing to the want of attention to the grace of God displayed in the gospel. There is no bar in the sinner's way to the Saviour, but what arises from a carnal heart; such as impenitency for sin, an attachment to self-righteousness, and an aversion to the perfections of God and his sovereign methods of grace.

But let it be observed, that a grant to come to Christ does not support a *claim*, or give a right to conclude they shall be saved by him. No, such a conclusion is only inferable from our having really believed in his name; a right to go to Christ is no proof we have done so.* What *evinces* a person's being a true believer is quite distinct from what *warrants* his applying to the Saviour: the latter arises from what God in his word says to him; the former appears from the change which is wrought in him. To put persons, therefore, upon examining themselves whether they have faith, before they believe, is extremely injudicious; and to encourage professors in the persuasion they are believers, without Scripture evidence of an internal change, is awfully dangerous.

It would be a great advantage to the discouraged, as well as to the presumptuous, to have right ideas of what it is to believe to the saving of the

---

* These two things cannot be too clearly distinguished. Many, perhaps, perish through confounding them. Ascertaining that they have the *warrant to apply* to Christ, they rest satisfied without actual application; and yet take to themselves the consolations which belong only to those who have applied. Let the reader take the following illustration of the case: I receive a card of invitation to a sumptuous entertainment; and this card is my *warrant* for attending it. But I may have this warrant, and yet never participate in the provisions of the feast;—these are for those only who *go* to it. I must *go* to the entertainment, and then the invitation I have received insures for me a participation of the provisions. J. A. W.

soul. Faith is a belief of the Divine testimony. For he that believeth not, maketh God a liar. Faith in Christ is a crediting what the Scriptures assert concerning him; which may be comprised in the following three things; *That* he is,—*what* he is,—and *whose* he is.

The first is absolutely necessary; for, saith Jesus, "Except ye believe that I am he," viz. the real and true Messiah, the promised Saviour, "ye shall die in your sins." But it is not enough to believe this, which wicked men may do; Simon the sorcerer did, and devils believe it and tremble. These evil spirits knew him to be Christ the Son of the living God. Luke iv. 41.

But true faith consists in believing likewise, *what he is.* Truths, respecting his person, offices, works, and relations, may be assented to by such as have no faith in his excellency, but have an enmity against what he is. But to them that believe Christ is precious; he is declared to be the chief among ten thousand, and altogether lovely. His personal qualities, with the nature and design of his work and offices, the real Christian believes. He gives credit to the Divine testimony, not only in respect of its reality, but likewise its holy *nature* and spiritual tendency. The tidings concerning the person of Christ, and his infinite fullness of merit and grace, are declared to be good, as well as true; and the renewed soul believes them to be so, even the only satisfying portion that an immortal mind can possess. He receives them as every way suited to his present circumstances, as guilty and impure; being divinely adapted to render him holy and happy for ever. This is what the Scripture calls an embracing, when true faith is the subject under immediate consideration. See Heb. xi. 13.

Saving faith is differently denominated in Scripture, but always exactly corresponding with the various representations of Christ in the gospel. Is he lifted up as an object to be beheld? Believers "look to him" as the wounded Jews did to the brazen serpent lifted up in the wilderness for their relief. Is he a "gift?" Faith as such "receives" him. As he is called the "bread of life," believing is termed an "eating or living upon" him. Considering him as a support, faith is described as a leaning upon him. He is called a faithful friend; and faith is then denominated a "confiding or trusting" in him. He is set forth as a "refuge," and faith is then termed a "running or flying" to him for safety. He is represented as the husband of his people, and then their faith is called giving themselves to him.

Many more instances might be produced of the diversification of believing in Christ, according as its object is represented; for the purpose of setting forth the various infinite blessings in him, and benefits flowing from Him, who is the real believer's all in all. But I hope the above few instances may suffice to illustrate the true Christian's belief in Jesus respecting *what he is;* with which faith salvation is inseparably connected in the Scriptures of truth.

As to faith in the third sense, i. e. *Whose he is:* Faith, or believing in the last sense, if right, must be founded on the Divine word as well as the former; for that must sink which has not "Thus saith the Lord" for its support. If faith be a belief of the Divine testimony, then the grand inquiry ought to be, who the Scriptures declare to be interested in Christ? To enforce the solemn inquiry, and lead to solid satisfaction in a manner so infinitely important, we may observe two things, which will readily be granted by every person of common understanding.

1. All men are not savingly interested in Christ, for some are declared to be none of his.

2. No man is described as belonging to Christ by his personal name, situation, profession, connexions, or descent.

Who then have a right, according to Scripture, to conclude Christ is theirs, and they are his? Some reply, *Christ belongs to those who believe themselves savingly interested in him.* But the query returns, On what is such a faith or belief founded? If their right to Christ arise from believing him to be theirs, they had no title to him before they so believed; therefore the thing was *false* when they first believed it *true;* and it is very extraordinary indeed that a falsehood should become a truth, by its being confidently believed, or industriously propagated. Faith makes no alteration in the nature of the thing believed. What is true does not become false because it is discredited. Nor is it possible that a *lie* should change its nature, and become true, however a person may strive to keep up a firm persuasion of its being a truth, and labor against doubting its reality.

It might be happy for such professors, whose faith is founded on falsehood, if they could be made ashamed of their assurance, by a deep conviction that they believe a lie, and rejoice in a thing of nought. 2 Thess. ii. 11; Amos vi. 13. In this condition, those most certainly are, who believe Christ is theirs without any Scriptural evidence to support the persuasion. But alas! the bands of such are generally made strong by the joy that accompanies their confidence: for they apply to themselves the promises of salvation, and think it would be a sin to doubt of their safety, and a much greater to cast away their confidence, which they apprehend will meet with a great recompense of reward. Such despise all evidences of a change of heart, and of the disposition of the soul, as legal and low: the maxim is, *The weaker the evidence the stronger the faith.*

Some of the class referred to have defined faith to consist in a believing that *Christ died for my sins.* Such a definition, to be sure, is consistent enough with the sentiment of universal redemption. For all who believe that doctrine must have such a faith, unless they should doubt their being of the human species. But if this sentiment be granted, the salvation of no man can be inferred from an interest in the Saviour's death, because those in hell (if it be allowed any of the human race are there) may with as much truth as those in heaven, say, *Jesus loved me and gave himself for me.* Such a faith is, therefore, destitute of evidence of a saving interest in Christ.*

Others have asserted that faith is a believing

---

* The belief that Christ died for my sins in particular corresponds with Universalism, for all Universalists must believe that Christ died for their sins in particular. And if any sinners of the human race are in the world of misery, they too, may, if Universalism be, on this point, correct, believe that Christ died for *their* sins in particular. Hence, the belief that he so died for my sins does not secure my salvation; for some who are not saved, may believe the very same, and hence I may be lost as well as they. This faith, then, is not that which saves the soul. J. A. W.

Christ to be a person's own. Be not discouraged, ye seeking souls, with the boasted attainments of such believers as aforesaid, who glory in their freedom from doubts about their soul's salvation. You have a more sure word of prophecy, to which ye do well to take heed, as to a light shining in a dark place. God has given, in his word, a full description of all those who are interested in Christ, and are, as such, heirs of his salvation; and those who answer the description have a right to conclude, that *through the grace of the Lord Jesus they shall be saved.* Those who have not the spirit of the Lord Jesus Christ, however they may make their boast of God, as the carnal Jews did, are none of his. Rom. viii. 9. "They that are Christ's have crucified the flesh with the affections and lusts." Gal. v. 24. They give full consent to the death of sin, and heartily cry respecting all their iniquities, Away with them, crucify them. They wish every sin to be the object of universal contempt, and would gladly put them to open shame. They account them the worst enemies to God and their souls; and such is their enmity against those grand deceivers, that nothing can satisfy them short of their total destruction.

The Spirit of God in the word, in describing the character of real saints, beareth witness with our spirit which are conscious of a real change, "that we are the children of God; and if children, then heirs; heirs of God, and joint heirs with Christ." Rom. viii. 16, 17. Therefore, "he that believeth on the Son of God, hath the witness in himself." That is, he is conscious of the acts of his own soul, that they are in *nature* and *kind*, however they are deficient in *degree*, what the people of God in the Scriptures are described by.

Every Christian, therefore, habitually believes that such persons as answer to the description of saints, whether themselves or others, shall have everlasting life, and that none but such shall be saved. He that believeth not God, hath made him a liar; because he believeth not the record that God gave of his Son. "And this is the record, that God hath given to us eternal life, and this life is in his Son." 1 John v. 10, 11. There is a cordial believing in Christ respecting both, *that he is*, and *what he is*, and likewise respecting *whose he is*, in reference to the true character of those interested in him, before the believer may be fully satisfied respecting his own personal claim to Christ.

Paul, writing to the saints at Ephesus, and speaking of himself and others who trusted in Christ, adds, "In whom ye also trusted, after that ye heard the word of truth, the gospel of your salvation. In whom also *after* that ye believed, ye were sealed with that Holy Spirit of promise." Eph. i. 13. The saints were not confirmed in their personal interest in the promises, till after they trusted, or believed in Christ.

Another apostle, in a letter to the people of God in general, says, "These things have I written unto you that believe on the name of Son of God; that ye may *know* that ye have eternal life, and that ye may believe on the name of the Son of God." 1 John v. 13. He had in the letter laid down several marks, by which the saints are distinguished from others; such as obedience to God, hatred to sin, and love to the brethren; and hereby (says he) we know that we know him. 1 John ii. 3. The weak among them, whom he called little children, he was confident, from the appearance of real holiness in them, were in a happy and safe condition, having their sins forgiven for Christ's sake. Yet these were not fully confirmed, though they had believed to the saving of the soul; therefore, what he had wrote for their serious consideration, was in order that they might be assured of eternal life, being included among those of whom he speaks in the preceding verse, "That have the Son."

He supposes some professors might "believe without evidence," and boldly say, "we have fellowship with God." 1 John i. 6. Says another

"I know him;" chap. ii. 4; "and abide in him," verse 6. "I love God;" chap. iv. 20. Yea, he supposes some professors might boast of having attained to *sinless* perfection; chap. i. 8 But without any ceremony he pronounces all those who claim a title to salvation, without evidence of sanctification, to be self-deceived, and strangers to God and truth. Chap. i. 6; ii. 10; iv. 20.

Every true Christian is possessed of what Jesus terms an *honest heart.* Luke viii. 15. They would not, they dare not claim, or take possession of what is not their own; they are persuaded that those who do, will be rejected at last, and made ashamed of their hope and presumptous persuasion. A God of truth can never require any man to believe a falsehood; nor even any thing relating to a fact which is unrevealed. For instance, he requires men to believe there are three that bear record in heaven, and that these three are one; and the union of two natures in the person of Christ. But *how* these are one, being not revealed, is neither the object of faith, nor the subject of human understanding. The support of faith is the authority of God. Hence the Scriptures are called "the faithful word," Tit. i. 9; "the true saying of God." Rev. xix. 9. "And this is a faithful saying," (to be depended upon as an established fact,) "and worthy of all acceptation," (being fully proved to be infinitely good as well as true,) "that Christ Jesus came into the world to save sinners." 1 Tim. i. 15.

Faith therefore includes not only an assent to gospel truths, but a persuasion of their infinite worth and transcendent glory; and personal interest therein ariseth from the evidence of having received the truth in the love of it; for faith, objectively considered, or as it respects the things believed by the Christian, is the compendium, or substance of things hoped for, as published in the glorious gospel of the grace of God. Faith, subjectively considered, consists in the evidence of things not seen by the carnal mind, or corporeal eye. Heb. xi. 1. These hidden realities, though concealed from the wise and prudent, are revealed unto babes. Matt. xi. 25. Every one who really receives Christ Jesus the Lord, to them he gives power, or authority, to become the sons of God, even to them that believe on his name. However weak their faith may be, they are possessed of that which in its own nature is an evidence that they are born not of blood, nor of the will of the flesh, nor of the will of man, but of God. John i. 12, 13.

But though every heaven-born soul is the subject of what evidences a relation to God, he has not always light enough to discern it.

Besides, a view of the depravity of his heart frequently fills him with fear that he is not passed from death unto life.

Such persons are referred to the following chapter.

CHAPTER II.

CONCERNING THE NEW BIRTH.

SOME gracious people are greatly discouraged because they cannot ascertain the time when they passed under such a change. They are persuaded of the truth, and are convinced of the propriety of the Lord's solemn asseveration, "Verily, verily, I say unto thee, except a man be born again, he cannot see (enter into) the kingdom of God." John iii. 3. But not knowing the time when they were born again, and perhaps, through confused ideas of what is intended by the term, they are kept in a state of uncomfortable suspense, and their progress in vital religion is retarded, not knowing how to determine whether they are, or are not, born again. To such persons I would propose the following considerations:

Do you know the exact time of your natural birth? None do from their own knowledge and memory; and though some cannot even obtain information on what day, or even in what year they were born, yet they do not doubt of the fact. As effects in natural things lead back to their respective causes, and are infallible proofs of their reality, so it is in spiritual affairs. In this manner we are taught in Scripture to proceed, in order to gain assurance respecting facts which fall not under immediate personal observation. Saith the apostle, "every house is builded by some man;" and as every structure is proof of human agency, so saints being God's workmanship, created anew in Christ Jesus, and habitations of God through the Spirit, the nature of the change produced in them proves Jehovah to be its author. Heb. iii. 4.

The great inquiry should be, Whether we are the subjects of the heavenly birth or not? for the time when, is an immaterial circumstance. As it is not necessary to know the time of your natural birth, in order to prove your proper humanity, neither is the knowledge of the time of your spiritual birth at all needful to evidence your true Christianity; the change may be evident, though the time when it commenced be uncertain.

To know whether a person is born again, it should be considered that the work of the Spirit of God upon the soul, whereby sinners are denominated new creatures, is set forth by figurative language. As there are new principles or dispositions produced, it is called a creation. "Created in Christ Jesus." Eph. ii. 10. As it bears resemblance to procreation, it is therefore called a regeneration and a new birth. These terms are used for the purpose of illustrating its nature, the evident and plain import of which are to point out, that a person who is the subject of such a gracious change, feels and views himself to be in such circumstances, in a spiritual sense, as resemble the natural condition of an infant; for such persons feel themselves feeble and forlorn; they are convinced of their utter inability to provide for the least of their numerous wants, or even to describe them: like a new-born babe, they desire the sincere milk of the word, which they relish, and are nourished by. They are dependent entirely on the Lord's care and kindness, who loves them, deals tenderly with them, feeds them with what is convenient for them, as they are able to bear it, clothes them with the robe of righteousness, and garments of salvation. He teaches them, gradually, the things relating to the kingdom of grace into which they are brought, and of which they are naturally ignorant; for "they shall all be taught of God, from the least of them to the greatest of them." Isaiah liv. 13. As they have a disposition for spiritual activity, so the Lord increases their strength, takes them by the hand, teaches them to go. Hosea xi. 3. As they grow in acquainance with their heavenly Father, and the household of faith, they feel a love to God, a fear of him, have their dependence upon him, and are desirous of his presence, protection, and guidance. They love all the people of God, and those the best who, as they think, most resemble him.

Those, therefore, who are thus dependent upon God, and have a relish for Divine things, or dispositions towards God of a filial nature, have the evidences of being born again, having been brought with godly simplicity to receive the kingdom of heaven as a little child. Luke xviii. 17.

The feeble and forlorn condition of the Jews, when God first entered into covenant with them, and they became his special property and care, is illustrated by an infant, in the most deplorable condition. Ezek. xvi. So the spiritual experiences of his people, both sorrowful and sweet, are represented by the metaphor of a helpless infant, under the kind care of its loving, compassionate, and prudent parent. Such bear the likeness of their Father God. As by their first birth they partake of the image of the earthly, so by their second birth they are made partakers of the heavenly; for that which is born of the flesh, is flesh; and that which is born of the Spirit, is spirit. John iii. 6. They that are born again, love what God loves, and hate what he abhors, which gradually increaseth as they grow in grace to maturity, as perfect men in Christ Jesus. A holy disposition is therefore an infallible proof of a heavenly descent.

CHAPTER III.

SPIRITUAL JOYS.

MANY Christians are discouraged on account of not having been favored with such strong consolations as others speak of; and some are stumbled because of the short duration of their joy; and in both the above cases perplexities arise about the real difference between false and true pleasures attending religion. Such persons should consider, that it is not the height of consolation, nor the length of its continuance, which proves it genuine. Some of the Galatian church, of whose gracious state the apostle was in doubt, spoke of great blessedness. Gal. iv. 15. The Israelites sang God's praise with great delight at the Red Sea, but soon forgot his works, and rebelled against his authority; the stony ground hearers received the word with joy, but not having depth of root, when tribulation came for the word's sake, their pleasure and profession died. Even Herod heard John with gladness, yet clave to his sins; and Ezekiel was a pleasant song to many of his hearers who took no delight in obedience to God.

Some may hold fast their self-deception, and go down to hell rejoicing in a thing of nought; for a hope of deliverance from punishment cannot fail to give pleasure; and while the pleasing expectation is supported, the degree of consolation arising from a false hope may be equal, yea, superior to what is produced by a good one. Such not knowing their own hearts, and the infinite evil of sin, are not plagued like other men. Psal. lxxiii. 5, 14. We ought seriously to consider from what our comforts spring, and in what they terminate, in order to know and judge of their true nature and kind: false comforts frequently arise from a partial view of God's salvation. An unsanctified soul will rejoice in the hope of a deliverance from the punishment of sin, simply from the principle of self-love. But mere safety does not satisfy the truly gracious; all such likewise want to have the power of sin subdued, and the pollution of sin removed; their habitual prayer to God is, "Take away all iniquity, and receive us graciously." Hosea xiv. 1, 2.

Pleasures arising from a prospect of freedom from sorrow, may be where sin maintains a full dominion; "I shall have peace, though I walk in the imagination of mine heart, to add drunkenness to thirst." Thus he blesseth himself in his heart, when he heareth Jehovah's tremendous curse.

How awful is Heaven's language to such a daring deluded sinner! "The Lord will not spare him, but the anger of the Lord and his jealousy shall smoke against that man, and all the curses that are written in this book shall lie upon him." Deut. xxix. 19, 20.

False joy sometimes arises from the *manner* of relief being brought to the mind; but true pleasure springs from the *matter* applied, or the nature and suitableness of truth discovered. The suddenness of relief is only a circumstance in itself, and yet some build their hope of salvation upon it; but those who infer that such impressions are all of God, and absolutely safe, forget that Satanical influences are compared to darts: on the other hand, some unmercifully censure every extraordinary relief as diabolical. But times of dreadful temptations and overwhelming sorrows are periods which will not admit of delay; and when viewed in that light, it is no wonder the soul with holy vehemence should cry, "make haste, make no tarrying, Oh my God." And, is it a wonder that God should hear prayer, or be found a present, yea, a very present help in time of trouble? If not, why then should such appearances be opposed or doubted? The Lord flies on the wings of the wind for the help of Jeshurun, and may he not avenge his own elect, who cry unto him day and night, and that speedily, though he may seem to bear long with them; for as he sendeth forth his commandment upon earth, his word runneth very swiftly? Yea, he says, "Before they call, I will answer: and whilst they are yet speaking, I will hear." Isaiah lxv. 24. Daniel found this promise verified in his experience; for while he was speaking in prayer, Gabriel being caused to fly swiftly, touched him, and told him, that at the beginning of his supplication, the commandment came forth, in obedience to which he appeared in his favor. Dan. ix. 21, 23.

Those, therefore, are not to be censured or discouraged, who have found that ere they were aware their souls were made like the chariots of Amminadab; provided their hope leads to holiness, and their peace and pleasure terminate in purity. Many christians have reason to admire the speedy manner in which the Lord has relieved them, when their prospects were dismal, and their souls with horror stood trembling on the brink of eternal woe; like a poor criminal at the fatal tree, expecting every moment to launch into eternity, but who is happily prevented by the sudden arrival of a reprieve or a pardon from his gracious sovereign. He admires and is thankful for the speed with which the joyful message came. Notwithstanding which, he does not consider the manner of the messenger's arrival; but the tidings brought are the principal spring of his joy, and the only foundation of his present security. The posts which carried the cruel edict from the Persian court, to destroy the Jews in every province were hastened by the king's commandment, as well as those despatched in their favor, therefore, the monarch's intention was not from thence discoverable. The speed with which a message is carried does not prove it to be of a favorable nature, nor does it so much as demonstrate *from* or to whom it is sent.

Neither does the *manner* in which any portion of Scripture is brought to the mind, determine its being the language of God to that person in particular; the mere mode of impressions is not essential to spiritual comfort, conviction, or instruction. Yet many are encouraged or cast down more from the *manner* in which impressions are made on their minds, than from the matter expressed, or the nature and tendency of truth contained in the Scriptures. A genuine hope in God, or the enjoyment of pardon, is ever accompanied with self-diffidence; such as are so favored, rejoice in Christ Jesus, and put no confidence in the flesh. Sacred pleasure is not only incomparably superior, but of a nature opposite to levity and carnal security; fervent love to God will be excited and promoted by it. I will, says David, love the Lord, because he hath heard my supplication; and of Mary it is said, she loved much because much was forgiven her. It invigorates repentance; "they shall look upon me whom they have pierced, and mourn," yea, "shall be ashamed and confounded when I am pacified towards them, for all that they have done, saith the Lord." It promotes humble, cheerful, and universal obedience; the language of such a soul is, "What am I? or what was my father's house, that thou shouldst bring me hitherto? How is it, Lord, thou shouldest thus manifest thyself! What shall I render unto the Lord? I will run the ways of thy commandments. Bless the Lord, O my soul."

In regard to those who are distressed about the fluctuation of their enjoyments, it may be a relief to their minds to consider that God "went up from Jacob, in the place where he talked with him." Gen. xxxv. 13. David's mountain stood strong, but when the Lord hid his face, he was troubled. Permanent joy is not to be expected in this world, but is reserved for the next. What God imparts now, is designed to encourage and forward the christian in his duty, and thus to profit rather than to please. The shorter our present comforts are, the oftener should we apply to the God of all consolation for the renewal of them; saying with

David, "Restore unto me the joys of thy salvation;" and with the pensive prophet, "O the hope of Israel, the Saviour thereof in time of trouble, why shouldest thou be as a stranger in the land, and as a wayfaring man, that turneth aside to tarry for a night?" Jer. xiv. 8. And the more watchful should we be lest we grieve the Holy Spirit, the Comforter, and cause him to withdraw his soul-cheering influences.

CHAPTER IV.

INDWELLING SIN.

A DEEP sense of internal depravity, or the prevalency of sin in the heart, has often been very stumbling to serious christians, who, on a view of their vileness, have been ready to conclude their cases are both singular and sad; "If I be a christian, why am I thus?"

It may be an advantage for such to reflect, that a soul-humbling sense of sin, and deep abasement before God, has been experienced by the most eminent saints recorded in Scripture. "Behold I am vile, I abhor myself." "I am undone. I am a man of unclean lips." "I blush to look up to heaven." "I am as a beast before thee." "Surely I am more brutish than any man, and have not the understanding of a man." "In me, that is, in my flesh, dwelleth no good thing. I am carnal, and sold under sin. I find a law in my members warring against that in my mind, leading me into captivity." "Iniquities prevail against me." "Evil is present with me. I cannot do the things that I would. O wretched man that I am!

who shall deliver me?" "We are all as an unclean thing."

These, with many more instances which might be produced, demonstrate, that true believers, and they only, are properly acquainted with the plague of their own hearts. Why then should the christian be discouraged through feeling himself to be, what those, who were eminent for godliness, have with shame and sorrow acknowledged they were? Besides, have you not repeatedly entreated the Lord to search and try you, to discover what was in your hearts? And shall you now be stumbled and discouraged because he has heard and answered your prayers; and as God has given you an experience similar to what was once the case of those who are now the subjects of spotless purity and perpetual praise, is it reasonable to conclude from thence you are not the subjects of a gracious change? You may rather infer, that if the Lord had been pleased to have slain you, he would not have shown you such things as these.

Remember the whole need not a physician, but those that are sick; and grace has made rich provision for healing all the diseases and maladies of the mind. Perhaps every good man will account himself of all others the most indebted to God and grace; for he feels that in himself which he does not certainly know is in any other, for every heart only knows its own bitterness. By such experiences, the Lord is training his people for the future glory. For, accounting themselves, as Paul did, the chief of sinners, 1 Tim. i. 15, their own salvation will be the matter of eternal wonder, every one viewing his own deliverance as the effect of a peculiar exertion of Divine power, and an uncommon display of rich superabounding grace. Being each under infinite deficiency, respecting their personal endeavors to extol the great Jehovah, mutual assistance will be intreated in the work of praise; for the language of the redeemed of the Lord to fellow saints frequently is, "O magnify the Lord with me, and let us exalt his name together." Psalm xxxiv. 3.

Go on, then, ye blessed of the Lord, pressing after the full possession of that salvation of which you see the absolute need, even a complete deliverance from sin, as well as from sorrow; that grace which has rendered sin loathsome, and Christ lovely in your view, is sufficient for you. In a perpetual dependence on which, may you hold on your way with courage and caution, till you arrive at Zion's celestial gate! Then shall you obtain ioy and gladness, and sorrow and sighing shall flee away. Isaiah xxxv. 10.

CHAPTER V.

ERRONEOUS VIEWS OF CHRISTIAN DOCTRINES.

The progress of another class of christians is retarded by a false and discouraging representation of the distinguishing doctrines of grace: which are frequently asserted to be inimical to experimental religion, and of such a nature as to supersede personal holiness, and render internal conformity to God unnecessary.

Whatever God has revealed in his word, we may be sure is worthy of himself, and advantageous to his people. We ought diligently to inquire what Jehovah has revealed as matter of faith and obedience; and whatever is of a divine origin demands our reverent attention, cordial reception, and cheerful obedience. It is the height of arrogance in a puny mortal to dispute with his Maker about the propriety of what he does or says. "O man, who art thou that repliest against God?" Rom. ix. 20. For the relief of such serious minds as are perplexed and stumbled in consequence of the aforesaid objections, let us briefly consider those doctrines which are generally supposed the most exceptionable in relation to christian experience.

First. The doctrine of imputation. This is not justly liable to the aforesaid objection; for the placing of the Redeemer's righteousness to the account of his people does not supersede the work of the Spirit of God in the soul, nor render unnecessary holiness of heart, or the exercises of spiritual graces. Imputation is not transfusion. It makes no alteration in the internal disposition. If it did, our sins being imputed to Christ would have tainted his holy mind. But though sin was placed to his account, and the Lord laid on him the iniquities of us all: though He was made sin for us, that he might legally suffer in our stead according to law; yet he was still the Holy One, who knew no sin as a principle in him. So Christ's righteousness "is unto all and upon all them that believe," Rom. iii. 22; by which they are freed from condemnation, but are not thereby made inwardly pure; the righteousness of Christ is not infused as a holy principle in them, but put upon them as a heavenly robe.

Now though righteousness delivers from death, and entitles to life, yet an internal disposition suited to the nature of heavenly felicity is absolutely necessary; therefore, there is need of a life of grace here, in order to a life of glory hereafter; and, indeed, they differ only in degree, not in nature and kind. Hence, Jesus says, "I give unto them eternal life." John x. 28. "This is life eternal, that they may know thee, the only true God, and Jesus Christ whom thou hast sent." John xvii. 3. Men need a righteousness *imparted*, as well as a righteousness *imputed;* the inner man of the heart is, therefore, created anew in righteousness and true holiness, in order to the enjoyment of true happiness. Being guilty, there was a necessity of Christ's fulfilling the law for us; but when perfect in holiness, the righteousness of the law will be fulfilled *in* us. By the former we escape eternal misery. By the latter we have a taste for, and are rendered capable of, enjoying heavenly felicity; therefore, we ought to be as much concerned to possess a *meetness* for heaven, as a *right* to it.

A capacity to enjoy does not give a title to enjoyment. A man, while sick, cannot enjoy the most pleasing inheritance. Yet no man in his right mind ever thought that the best state of health, or the firmest constitution, could give a title to an estate. So the believer's claim to future glory, or entitling righteousness, does not arise out of his own personal qualifications, though there is a necessity of perfect holiness, in order to complete happiness. "This is the heritage of the servants of the Lord; and their righteousness is of me, saith the Lord." Isaiah liv. 17. In answer to the solemn question, "Who shall ascend the hill of the Lord, and who shall stand in his holy place? it is said, "he that hath clean hands and a pure heart, he shall receive the blessing from the Lord, and righteousness FROM the God of his salvation." Psalm xxiv. 4, 5. The believer, therefore, longs for purity, but, after all his religious attainments, resolves to go through life, down to death, and home to glory "in the strength of the Lord God," saying, "I will make mention of thy righteousness, even of thine only." Psalm lxxi. 16.*

Second. Some are ready to object against the efficacious nature of Divine grace in conversion, and say "that constraining grace cannot be consistent with the natural freedom of the human will. For if I freely choose the things of God, how is my choice owing to divine grace? And if

---

* Justification and sanctification have each their own appropriate place in the Christian system. Both are absolutely indispensable, and of course neither is inimical to the other. Only let them be distinguished properly, and their harmony becomes obvious. Justification is by the imputation of Christ's righteousness. Sanctification is by the Spirit's operation on the heart. Justification is a *declaration* made *respecting* us; sanctification is a *work* wrought *in* us. Justification frees us from *condemnation;* sanctification cleanses us from *pollution.* Justification affects our *state* in point of *law;* sanctification improves our *condition* in point of *fact.* J. A. W.

I be impelled by the power of grace, how am I free in my choice?"

By proper attention to our experience of mental acts, whether as creatures or christians, it will be found that choosing is a preferring some persons or things above others. The preference or choice, is the effect of their appearing more agreeable, or having an ascendency to our esteem. However precious or excellent any thing be in itself, yet if that worth be not discovered, it does not become the object of choice.

Things are therefore chosen or refused, according as they are presented to the mind's view, as agreeable or disagreeable. Now, as the natural man cannot know the things of the Spirit of God, because they are spiritually discerned, therefore, he does not choose them. Their Divine beauty and spiritual excellency lie concealed from the carnal mind; therefore natural things are chosen or preferred to spiritual, being more agreeable to the mind in its unrenewed state. But when omnipotent grace begets new principles in the soul, and opens the understanding to behold things as they really are, then the world and all temporary good sinks into nothing and vanity, when compared with Christ and the blessings of the gospel. Now the will, which before freely chose sinful delights, as freely chooses the one thing needful.

Christ, in whom sinners saw no form nor comliness wherefore they should desire him, is now in their esteem the chief among ten thousand, and altogether lovely. Now they freely choose such things for their portion, and such persons for their associates, as before they had an utter aversion to. Now they as freely choose the paths of virtue and religion, as before they did those of vice and sensuality. If there be such an alteration experienced, need I ask such a happy soul, "Who maketh thee to differ?" 1 Cor. iv. 7. Surely such will be free to acknowledge with the apostle, "By the grace of God I am what I am." 1 Cor. xv. 10. If so, you cannot consistently object,

Thirdly; To the doctrine of election; for it looks upon you with a friendly aspect, and by it you are informed, that grace was treasured up for you in Christ Jesus before the world began; and if God has now given grace to you, the certain pledge of glory, it surely will not be offensive to be informed that he intended to do so, and that he had it in reserve for you before he bestowed it upon you.

You cannot complain of his having loved you too soon, or made gracious provision for you too early. No, you will admire and adore the free and distinguishing grace of the Father, who chose you from everlasting, set you apart for himself, preserved you in Christ Jesus, and by his Spirit called you with a high calling, and is now fitting you for the full enjoyment of "the salvation which is in Christ Jesus with eternal glory." 2 Tim. ii. 10. "Put on, therefore, (as the elect of God, holy and beloved,) bowels of mercies, kindness, humbleness of mind, meekness, long suffering," Col. iii. 12, which you are under the strongest obligations to discover to your fellow-christians and fellow-creatures. Ever remember that those who "are a chosen generation, a royal priesthood, an holy nation, a peculiar people, should show forth the praises of him who hath called them out of darkness into his marvellous light. 1 Pet. ii. 9.

This doctrine is not discouraging in its own nature, (however it may be represented,) to any sincere seeking sinner. Such are not called to produce evidences of their election, in order to warrant their application to Jesus for salvation. No, my dear friends, your present concern is now to have guilt and pollution removed, that you may stand accepted before Jehovah's bar. To you there is a fountain opened, the blood of Jesus, which cleanseth from all sin. Your desire of coming to Christ, under a sense of the absolute need you are in of a Saviour, is a hopeful sign that you shall know, if you follow on to know the Lord. None but the chosen of God do ever heartily choose religion as the one thing needful; and the language of the compassionate Saviour is, "all that the Father giveth me shall come to me; and him that cometh to me I will in nowise cast out." John vi. 37.

Therefore such as long and wait for the salvation of God, through sanctification of the spirit and belief of the truth as it is in Jesus, whose heart's desire, is to be found in Christ, and without blame before him in love, will never meet with a disappointment; for he who cannot lie hath said, "He will regard the prayer of the destitute, and not despise their prayer." Ps. cii. 17. He satisfieth the longing soul, even such as (for the present) sit in darkness, and in the shadow of death, being bound in affliction and iron. Ps. cvii. 9, 10. Cordially to embrace Christ, and deliberately to take up his cross and follow him, are the genuine effects of electing love. To every such soul the language of the Lord is, "Yea, I have loved thee with an everlasting love: therefore with loving kindness have I drawn thee." Jer. xxxi. 3. "The Lord thy God in the midst of thee is mighty; he will save, he will rejoice over thee with joy; he will rest in his love; he will joy over thee with singing." Zeph. iii. 17.

You who love the Lord, and desire to be entirely and eternally devoted to him, you know and are sure you were not naturally so disposed; and if so, that new covenant promise made to Immanuel has been fulfilled in your favor. "Thy people shall be willing in the day of thy power." Ps. cx. 3. You who are conscious of having chosen and elected the Lord as your God, need not perplex yourself about his choice of you as his people. But know that the Lord has set apart him that is godly for himself. Ps. iv. 3. Therefore, blessed is the man whom the Lord hath chosen, and caused to approach unto him. Psalm lxv. 4. For the foundation of God standeth sure, having his seal, The Lord knoweth them that are his. 2 Tim. ii. 19.

This doctrine is a source of strong consolation to them who have fled for refuge to Christ, the hope set before them. Heb. vi. 17, 18. For in the midst of all the perplexing difficulties and trying occurrences in this fluctuating world, such may triumph in the hope of eternal life, which God that cannot lie promised them in Christ Jesus before the world began. Titus i. 2. For yet a little while, and he that hath said he shall come, will come and will not tarry; then shall they meet with a hearty welcome into the kingdom prepared for them from the foundation of the world.

Fourthly. If discouragements be removed respecting the doctrine of election, it is not probable that redemption will be viewed in a light unfavorable to weak Christians. Every truth relating to the law of God or the gospel of grace, if properly stated, will be disgustful to the carnal and unsanctified mind. But those who are Christians indeed, though they may be ignorant of, or even prejudiced against, the terms by which truths are distinguished; yet the nature of truth is not with them an object of aversion; as personal election is not prejudicial to such, it cannot be thought redemption should be so.

The election and redemption of men are inseparably connected in Scripture as distinct links in the grand chain of gospel truth. The personal objects and end are the same in each; and Christ's claim to his people is founded on both; "Thine they were, and thou gavest them me. I pray not for the world, but for them which thou hast given me, for they are thine. And all mine are thine, and thine are mine." John xvii. 6, 9, 10. As they were given to him, so they were purchased by him; they were committed to his care as sheep to a shepherd, and he laid down his life for them. John x. 15. "The church of God, which he hath purchased with his own blood," Acts xx. 28, called "the precious blood of Christ, as of a Lamb without blemish and without spot." 1 Pet. i. 19. They were given him "out of the world." John

xvii. 6. And he redeemed them "from among men." Rev. xiv. 4.

When God choose his people, he foreknew that man would fall, and the whole human race would lose their purity, and become transgressors from the womb. Isaiah xlviii. 8. He therefore chose them to complete salvation and purity, that they might be "without blame before him in love." Eph. i. 4. Christ in whom they were chosen, and to whose care they were committed, being constituted the Head of the church, he became the Saviour of the body, and "gave himself for it, that he might sanctify and cleanse it with the washing of water by the word: that he might present it to himself a glorious church, not having spot or wrinkle, or any such thing; but that it should be holy and without blemish." Eph. v. 25—27. Powerful operations of grace in and upon the church and chosen of God, by which they are purified and made meet for heaven, are necessarily connected with the redemption which Jesus obtained for them by his precious blood. Divine justice was satisfied with the stipulated price, and infinite power secures the purchased possession.

Such a redemption is suitable to Christians of every rank, and discouraging to none, if its nature be known properly, or what is included in it be duly considered.

Those who come to Christ consider themselves as criminals justly condemned, and therefore in absolute need of a pardon. 'God be merciful to me a sinner,' is the language of each; and where should such look for relief but to the Saviour, "in whom we have redemption through his blood, the forgiveness of sins, according to the riches of his grace?" Eph. i. 7. Gracious souls are conscious of having grievously departed from God. "All we, like sheep, have gone astray: we have turned every one to his own way." Isa. liii. 6. "All our righteousnesses are as filthy rags." Isa. lxiv. 6. But Jesus, to whom the flock belonged, has made satisfaction for the damage sustained; for "the Lord laid on him the iniquity of us all." His people know they have trespassed and are unable to make a recompense; for, being poor, they have nothing to give unto him against whom they have trespassed. Numb. v. 7. But in this doctrine Jesus is represented as the kind and compassionate kinsman who engaged, that for the trespass of his people a recompense should be made unto the Lord. He was therefore wounded for our transgressions, he was bruised for our iniquities, and "redeemed us from the curse of the law, being made a curse for us." Gal. iii. 13.

Do they consider themselves afar off from God, and desire to be a people near unto the Lord?

How cheering to such is the doctrine of redemption! Wherefore remember ye, said Paul to the saints in his day, that "ye were without Christ, being aliens from the commonwealth of Israel, having no hope, and without God in the world; but now in Christ Jesus, ye who sometimes were far off, are made nigh by the blood of Christ." Eph. ii. 12, 13. "For Christ also hath once suffered for our sins, the just for the unjust," not that he might only open, or put us into a way in which we might possibly attain to glory, but "that he might bring us to God." 1 Pet. iii. 18. In this the saints triumph in heaven, and of this they sing, saying, "Thou wast slain, and hast redeemed us to God by thy blood." Rev. v. 9. Cheer up ye discouraged souls, "for with the Lord there is mercy, and with him is plenteous redemption. And he shall redeem Israel from all his iniquities." Psalm cxxx. 7, 8.

The Redeemer's priesthood and power are unchangeable. "Wherefore he is able also to save them to the uttermost that come unto God by him, seeing he ever liveth to make intercession for them." Heb. vii. 24, 25. You who are now the servants of God, were once slaves to Satan and sin, serving divers lusts and pleasures; wherefore the great deliverance and happy change are entirely owing to the efficacy of redemption.

How thankful ought we to be, who are made free from such an awful state of bondage; "for as much as ye know that ye were not redeemed with corruptible things, as silver and gold, from your vain conversations received by tradition from your fathers, but with the precious blood of Christ." 1 Pet. i. 18.

That peculiar and particular redemption of which Christ is the author, cannot justly be deemed discouraging to any who are sensible of their misery, and long for deliverance; because those who are declared in Scripture to be personally interested in this special blessing, are described by qualities of mind and exercises of soul, many of which the weakest christian knows and feels himself to be the subject of; such as a conscious sense of spiritual depravity, debt, and danger, joined with an approbation of Jesus, and desires after those blessings which result from his merits and mediation.

Let saints rejoice in, and sinners seek, this great redemption, which consists in a deliverance "from the curse of the law," Gal. iii. 13; "from all iniquity," Tit. ii. 14; from "the works of the devil," 1 John iii. 8; from "bondage," Heb. ii. 15; from "the power of the grave," Hos. xiii. 14; and "from the wrath to come," 1 Thess. i. 10. From these considerations, the certain salvation of all the redeemed may be safely inferred, for the redemption is not only copious, but durable; for Jesus has "obtained eternal redemption for us." Heb. ix. 12. Therefore of the way of holiness it is asserted that "the redeemed shall walk there, and the ransomed of the Lord shall return, and come to Zion with songs, and everlasting joy upon their heads; they shall obtain joy and gladness, and sorrow and sighing shall flee away." Isaiah xxxv. 9, 10.

Fifthly. The doctrine of final perseverance can scarcely be a stumbling block to the saints, and none but such ought to hope they shall be saved. Those who enter upon a journey, and are very desirous of a safe arrival, will not count it a disadvantage to have a guide, who will watch over them night and day, and never leave them, but conduct them through every difficulty they may meet with. Is it reasonable to suppose they will be discouraged to hear that every thing is previously prepared by a kind friend that went on purpose, as their forerunner, for their accommodation while on the road, and their joyful entrance and welcome reception to those mansions where they wish to dwell for ever?

Would it sink the courage of a soldier, or cause dim to enter the field of battle with reluctance, because he is given to understand, that no one who draws the sword in favor of his sovereign shall be slain, but shall assuredly gain a glorious victory, and return with songs of triumph to the grand metropolis, and there in the midst of millions of joyful spectators receive every mark of honor and approbation which can be desired from the king?

The doctrine, if properly understood, cannot be disadvantageous to any man, though it be frequently abused, as every other part of revelation is, and likewise its Divine Author. It does not encourage sloth, or suppose the exercise of grace unnecessary, and render caution needless. No, it is "through faith and patience they inherit the promises." The intention and design of the great and precious promises are to encourage a close adherence to Christ, and a continuation in well doing, as connected with eternal life. And it is a stimulating motive not to be idle, when they know their labor shall not be in vain in the Lord. 1 Cor. xv. 58. To know that the doctrine is a truth, I need only say, Search the Scriptures, which testify of Christ's near relation to them: the strength of his love towards them; the infinite price he gave for them: the change he has wrought in them, and the declaration he has made concerning them, that where he is they shall be, and because he lives they shall live also.

CHAPTER VI.

PROVIDENCE.

MANY Christians are stumbled and discouraged because God's providences appear in various instances, to be contrary to his promises. To consider them as real opposites, the good man knows would be absurd. But not being able to reconcile them as relating to himself, he therefore is ready to conclude, that as *providences* are gloomy and appear against him, he has no right to interpret the *promises* of God in his favor. It may be a relief to such to observe,

First. Jehovah's proceedings are extremely mysterious. *His ways are in the sea, and his footsteps are not known.* As the Governor of the world, *clouds and darkness are round about him,* and the most penetrating creature cannot pry into his deep and vast designs. To impeach his conduct is the greatest insolence, to prescribe to him rules of propriety, is horrid presumption. We ought to "be still, and know that he is God," and does all things well; therefore as relating to *his* will and operations, we may truly say, *Whatever is, is best.*

The history of Joseph is a striking proof of the mystery of Providence; the Lord's kindness to him at last appeared, notwithstanding all the awful consequences attending his brethren's cruelty. Through ignominy he was brought to honor; through slavery, to liberty and authority; by means of a prison he was advanced to a palace. Let discouraged Christians wait with patience, till they see in what their trials terminate. When a decision is difficult and dangerous, a suspension of judgment is safe; therefore judge nothing before the time.

Second. Good and great men have frequently been mistaken when they have ventured to pass judgment on the proceedings of God. David thought he should one day die by the hand of Saul. Providence wore such a gloomy aspect, that he concluded the promises respecting him would never be accomplished. Jacob said of trying Divine dispensations, "All these things are against me." And yet those very providences brought him into such a state of honor, comfort and tranquillity, as he never before enjoyed. So awful and intricate were the Divine proceedings toward Job, that he appeared to his friends a singular object of God's displeasure. Yea, he himself verily thought that the Lord counted him as an enemy, and treated him as such. You who think there is no sorrow like unto your sorrow, attend to the lamentation of that man of God, which he uttered in the anguish of his spirit, and mark the complaint which Job made in the bitterness of his soul, ch. vii. from verse 3; ch. xiii. 24, 27; ch. xvi., and ch. xix. 6, 21. Jeremiah, who with remarkable courage pleaded on Heaven's behalf against a revolted nation, though he had sweet intercourse with the Most High, yet, through a complication of trying dispensations, said, "Surely against me is he turned." Lam. iii. 3. Such discouragements have not only attended some few individuals who have been called to bear the burden and heat of the day, but have accompanied the people of God in general. "Zion said, the Lord hath forsaken me, and my Lord hath forgotten me." Isa. xlix. 14.

The above, and many more instances of the like kind, are left on sacred record, for our admonition: these mournful proofs of human weakness serve to convince us of our incapacity to discover, in dark dispensations, the harmony and connexion between the kindness of God's heart, and the operations of his hand; likewise of the necessity of walking by faith, and not by sight. Those, therefore, "who are in darkness, and have no light," are graciously invited and encouraged to "trust in the name of the Lord, and stay themselves upon their God." "You have heard of the patience of Job, and have seen the end of the Lord, that the Lord is very pitiful and of tender mercy." May the discouraged christian come to the same resolution, which that eminent man of God did, saying, "Though he slay me, yet will I trust in him." Job xiii. 15.

Thirdly. By such trying providences the Lord discovers to his people what is in their hearts, Deut. viii. 2; their humility and repentance are promoted, and their dependence on God increased. They are put upon self-examination, in order to know why the Lord contendeth with them: each one, therefore, with solemn seriousness, is brought to interrogate conscience, saying, What have I done? And seeing the absolute necessity of direction, support, and pardon, they become more frequent and fervent in prayer. Like Jacob, they retire from the world to wrestle with God; and being encouraged by his precious promises, are, therefore, resolved not to let him go without a blessing; therefore, they cry unto him day and night, (Luke xviii.,) praying without ceasing. And many kind interpositions of Providence are recorded in Scripture, and are still experienced by his people, who have by adverse dispensations been stirred up to seek the Lord with their whole hearts. When Jacob wept and made supplication to his God, the terrible prospect of his brother's approaching him at the head of a furious army, breathing vengeance, was changed into a melting scene of tender friendship and affection. Esau's dreadful designs were at once dismissed; and instead of killing, he salutes his brother with kisses, and generously offers his service for his future protection.

Thus providences are in fact designed to fulfil the promises of God in a way which prepares the minds of his people for the reception of the favor he intends to confer. Thus God's wisdom, goodness, power, and veracity, become the object of admiration; for thereby the Lord makes crooked things straight, and rough places plain, humbles and yet helps, discovers the corruption of the human heart; and thus from a sense of meanness and misery, difficulty and danger, deliverances appear more conspicuously the effects of wonderful grace.

God trieth the righteous by a suspension of promised mercies, and such delays are often interpreted as denials, through the prevalency of unbelief. But let tried christians consider the conduct of Providence towards the heirs of promise, as recorded in Scripture, in order to the support of hope, and a patient waiting for Christ. Abraham was kept waiting five-and-twenty years, and then with joy embraced the promised son.

Promised mercies frequently are mistaken in their first appearance, through their being viewed by the eye of sense and reason, as clothed with the garb of misery. The choicest mercies have come in disguise; therefore who can by present appearances know what is good for a man in this life, which he spendeth as a shadow? Ecc. vi. 12. It is evident, from an impartial survey of Jehovah's conduct, that the methods he takes to accomplish his own gracious designs, and his people's holy desires, are worthy of himself, though frequently the very reverse of the plans of finite wisdom; as remarkably evidenced in his dealings with Abraham, Jacob, Joseph, Moses, David, Daniel, and many others whose religious characters shine as stars of the first magnitude, in the horizon of grace.

Fourthly. Another spring of perplexity respecting the providences of God, is, mistaken views of the nature of Divine promises. Spiritual blessings promised in the Scriptures are frequently construed as including certain degrees of temporal felicity. Such an interpretation prevailed among the disciples of Christ; and being disappointed in their hopes of such enjoyments, therefore, *sorrow filled their hearts*, the expectation of earthly dignity and worldly splendor beclouded their minds, and darkened their understandings respecting the spiritual glories of Christ, the nature of his kingdom, and designs of his death. Though there was an inconsistency and real contrariety in nature between the *proceedings* of God and his promises as interpreted by them, yet afterwards, when favored with a clearer understanding of the Scriptures, they saw a happy harmony, and an inseparable connexion between them, and rejoiced in the accomplishment of the promises of God, which were all found, yea, and amen, in Christ Jesus.

To prevent the like mistake among believers, the apostle to the Hebrews points out various trying providences attending the worthies of old; who wandered about in sheep skins and goat skins, being destitute, afflicted, tormented, but through faith and patience are now inheriting the promises. Therefore, having nothing of this world is not inconsistent with inheriting all things which relate to the world to come. The Lord has promised to provide for his people's real wants in this life. He hath said, "Thy bread shall be given, and thy water shall be sure;" "your heavenly Father knoweth you have need of these things." "He careth for you,"—but he hath not described the quality or quantity of earthly good, with which you shall be fed. Poverty, yea extreme poverty, has been the lot of many heirs of glory. The churches in Macedonia were in deep poverty. Yet many of the children of God were poorer than they to whose relief the said churches contributed, even beyond their power, of which the apostle Paul bears record, 2 Cor. viii. 1—5. "Uunto the church in Smyrna write these things, saith the first and the last, which was dead and is alive, I know thy works and tribulation and poverty, but thou art rich." Rev. ii. 8, 9.

"Hearken, my beloved brethren, hath not God chosen the poor of this world, rich in faith, and heirs of the kingdom, which he hath promised to them that love him?" Jam. ii. 5. The same inspired writer even supposes a brother or sister to be naked, and destitute of daily food, ver. 15. Such have therefore been spoken of by the appellation of *poor saints*. Rom. xv. 26. A distressed saint may lie at the door of a rich sinner without receiving a crumb of relief, and appear as if forsaken by God and man. But oh, how great the change! How vast the difference in eternity! He who seemed as if neglected by heaven and earth, ascends at death to glory and to Abraham's bosom; while the sumptuous liver sinks down to hell, and being in torment, asks in vain for a drop of water. But of Lazarus, it is said with an air of sacred pleasure, NOW *he is comforted*.

Fifthly. Some have great discouragements and perplexity, arising from the failure of what they have considered as special and direct promises made to them in particular, as relating to the path of duty, or the enjoyment of some future good. The persuasion of promises being made to them in particular, arose perhaps from some portion of Scripture being impressed on their mind, the terms and language of which were exactly suitable to what they had been seeking the Lord about, and therefore deemed expressive of his mind in that particular; and the failure of these, discourages their hope respecting the fulfilment of *those* which relate to their eternal salvation.

For the relief of such I observe, that though it is not denied but that, in some special cases the Lord may have favored some of his people with intimations of his mind in the manner aforesaid, nevertheless there is commonly danger and disappointment attending such a construction of Scripture in ordinary affairs; for we need no new revelation to point out the path of duty, the Scriptures being sufficient for such a purpose, and a more sure word of prophecy than anything referred to above. A criminal curiosity or anxiety to know future events, the Lord in mercy may reprove in his people, by disappointments. The design of the promises of God is to encourage faith and hope in the Lord, that he will provide what he sees necessary, and give what is good to those who fear him; but not to make a previous discovery in what *manner* he will support and supply. Even Moses, the man of God, seems to have been mistaken in regard to the time when, and the means by which the Lord intended to accomplish the deliverance of his people from the bondage of Egypt; for when he defended the injured Israelite, and avenged him that was oppressed, he supposed his brethren would have understood that God by his hand would have delivered them, but they understood not; Acts vii. 25. And instead of his being then embraced as a deliverer, he was informed against, and banished as a delinquent. He continued in a state of exile for forty years; and afterwards, when the Lord sent him from Midian to Pharaoh, to demand in his name Israel's release, instead of deliverance, their bondage was increased, and his conduct severely censured; on which account he returned unto the Lord, and said, "Lord, wherefore hast thou so evil entreated this people? Why is it that thou hast sent me? For since I came to Pharaoh to speak in thy name, he hath done evil to this people; neither hast thou delivered thy people at all;" Exod. v. 21—23. And when providences turned up contrary to what Jeremiah expected, he in the bitterness of his soul uttered these awful words: "O Lord, thou hast deceived me, and I was deceived." Jer. xx. 7.

From the above instances it is evident that persons may be in some cases disappointed in their most sanguine expectations in regard to the dispensations of God in this life, and yet the foundations of their hope remain unshaken in reference to eternal salvation. May christians be cautious, and not use the word of the Lord in such a manner, and for such purposes, as were never intended! To interpret the designs of God, from detached sentences, either impressed on the mind, or as first presented to the eye on opening the sacred volume, is very injudicious, and has an entangling tendency; therefore, as the apostle says, "We do not cease to pray for you, and to desire that ye might be filled with the knowledge of his will, in all wisdom and spiritual understanding." Col. i. 9. In order to which may you be enabled to compare spiritual things with spiritual; 1 Cor. ii. 13. "Let the word of Christ dwell in you in all wisdom." Col. iii. 16.

The mistakes of eminent saints are recorded, not for our imitation, but our admonition, and to prevent overwhelming despondency on viewing our own mistakes, and to show the necessity of a careful examination of ourselves, fervent application to God, humble dependence on him, cheerful obedience to him, and a patient waiting for him. "For whatsoever things were written aforetime, were written for our learning; that we, through patience and comfort of the Scriptures might have hope." Rom. xv. 4.

PART III.

PRACTICAL DIFFICULTIES.

CHAPTER I.

SINS OF PROFESSORS.

THE disposition and conduct of some professors of religion, is very stumbling to serious inquirers after the way in which they should walk.

First. A proud censorious spirit, condemning the weak as worthless, and treating inferiors with an air of contempt, is very trying and discouraging. But who hath despised the day of small things? God does not, therefore men ought not; and it is certain a humble christian cannot. Let the weak and discouraged christian contemplate the compassionate Saviour, who will not break the bruised reed, nor quench the smoking flax. The lambs he will lay in his bosom, and gently lead those that are with young, and to them who have no might he will increase strength; the strongest believer was once a babe in Christ; the tallest cedar once was not superior to the lowest shrub; and the stoutest oak was once in as tender a state as a feeble straw. How unreasonable then to despise the weak, seeing that those who have arrived to the highest eminence in religion, in their beginnings were but small. Those, therefore, who are strong, ought to bear the infirmities of the weak, and not to please themselves. Support the weak, is the Lord's express command. Hence, says the apostle, "let us not therefore, judge one another any more, but judge this rather, that no man put a stumbling-block, or an occasion to fall, in his brother's way." Rom. xiv. 13.

Secondly. Loose professors are extremely pernicious; of such the apostle spoke with weeping, and pronounced them enemies to the cross of Christ. By them saints are discouraged and sinners hardened, the good ways of God are evil spoken of, religion reproached, the righteous traduced, and the name of the Lord blasphemed. When professors fall into sin, the cry of the profane is, *this is their religion.* But the established christian with sighing says; no, such miscarriages are owing to its absence. Weak believers are not only grieved, but silenced and confounded: and when those who are eminent for God are overcome by the deceitfulness of sin or the violence of temptation, christians in general are alarmed, as when a standard-bearer fainteth; and some are thereby for a time so discouraged, that they dare not profess* religion, fearing they should likewise act an unbecoming part, and deeper wound its reputation. Thus they linger, though they love, not daring to proceed for fear of falling. Others, to avoid being sharers in reproach, sigh and go backwards into a state of pretended neutrality.

Some notorious transgressors, termed *sinners in Zion*, when reproved for their sins, and admonished according to the Scriptures, and especially such as are excluded from church communion on account of their abominations, will, from a spirit of revenge, join affinity with the world, and Satan like, turn accusers of the brethren with whom they were connected, and speak of them all manner of evil. Such apostates will frequently dress up the imperfections of professors of religion, so as to gratify the taste

* This reason for not professing religion, though often assigned, is entirely without force. A Christian must live without professing religion till his dying hour, if he would be *quite certain* that he shall not afterwards dishonor his profession. And, moreover, it is sinning to avoid sin; "doing evil that good may come;"—for certainly it is sin to disobey the commands of Christ by not confessing him before men. And such a course is presumptuous; for God has promised "to meet them that rejoice and work righteousness; them that remember him *in his ways*." To be secure, then, against declension, backsliding, and apostacy, we must be found *in his ways*, and not expect Him to go out of his way to meet us. J. A. W.

of the ungodly, to whom the sins of the saints afford high entertainment, and on which they feast with satisfaction. "They eat up the sin of my people, and they set their heart on their iniquity." Hos. iv. 8, 9. In consequence of which those who sigh for the abounding abominations of the land, and are active for God in Zion, become the derision of fools, and the song of the drunkard.

Such things are very trying; but shall religion be deserted because it is dishonored? No, God forbid; the Lord's cause is good and honorable. Christ and religion are no worse for being betrayed, denied, or misused. Shall the rebellion of some be urged in favor of our disloyalty? Ought we to be inactive because others are indolent? Or not be true, because they are treacherous? When Christ was deserted by pretended friends, he addressed his few remaining followers thus: "Will ye also go away?" To which Peter replied in the name of the rest, "Lord, to whom should we go? thou hast the words of eternal life."

May every lover of Jesus be in like manner resolved to adhere to him! How rational, how becoming the determination in every point of view! For Jesus is possessed of every thing relating to eternal life: he, and he only, can satisfy and save the immortal soul. Is sin dreaded as aforesaid? Let such consider which is the most likely method to be kept from its prevalency. Surely those whose daily cry is, Hold me up, and then I shall be safe, cannot with calmness conclude, that those are most likely to be heard of God and kept from sin, who disregard his authority, and live in the neglect of duty. A prevailing sense of weakness is no indication of danger; no, pride goeth before destruction, and a haughty spirit before a fall.

The christian ought to consider, that the fewer they are that engage heartily in the cause of real religion, and the greater the opposition made to it, the more is his assistance needed. May such resolve "to go in the strength of the Lord God, making mention of his righteousness, and of his only." Though you proceed with trembling steps, the Lord can make you say and sing with holy triumph, "The bows of the mighty men are broken, and they that stumbled are girt with strength." 1 Sam. ii. 4. "The God of Israel is he that giveth strength and power unto his people; blessed be God." Ps. lxviii. 35.

Those who continue cool spectators, caring for none of these things, would do well to consider that the Lord allows no neutrality in the important and perpetual contest between the kingdom of heaven and that of hell, but says, he that is

16*

not for us is against us. He abhors indifference in matters of religion. "I would thou wert cold or hot; so then because thou art lukewarm, and neither cold nor hot, I will spew thee out of my mouth." Rev. iii. 15, 16. How alarming the language in Deborah's song! "Curse ye Meroz, curse ye bitterly the inhabitants thereof, because they came not to the help of the Lord, to the help of the Lord against the mighty." Judg. v. 23. May the supine Christian hear and fear!

CHAPTER II.

ENMITY OF THE WORLD.

SOME are stumbled on account of the reproach and persecution attending religion. A prospect of suffering in person, property, or character, is grievous to nature and trying to grace.

In regard to reproaches from men, we may observe, those who do not deserve them, need not dread them. "If ye be reproached for the name of Christ, happy are ye, for the spirit of glory and of God resteth upon you; on their part he is evil spoken of, but on your part he is glorified." 1 Pet. iv. 14. "Cruel mockings, reproaches, and persecutions" have been the lot of the righteous in every age, who are generally called to endure a great fight of afflictions as soon as they are illuminated, partly whilst they are made a gazing-stock, both by reproaches and afflictions, and partly whilst they become companions of them who are so used. Heb. x. 33. If any man will live godly in Christ Jesus, he must suffer persecution; for as of old, he that was born after the flesh persecuted him that was born after the Spirit, even so it is now. Gal. iv. 29.

But though such treatment is very trying, yet how much more dreadful are the frowns of God and the stings of conscience. Jehovah's smiles will infinitely outweigh the revilings of men, or the rage of the devil; yet a little while, and the wicked shall cease from troubling, and the weary shall be at rest. "Hearken unto me, (saith the Lord,) ye that know righteousness, the people in whose heart is my law. Fear ye not the reproach of men, neither be ye afraid of their revilings, for the moth shall eat them up like a garment, and the worm shall eat them like wool; but my righteousness shall be for ever, and my salvation from generation to generation." Isa. lviii. 7, 8. Attend, O discouraged christian, to the Saviour's cheering language, "Blessed are ye when men shall hate you, and when they shall separate you from their company, and shall reproach you, and cast out your name as evil, for the Son of man's sake. Rejoice and leap for joy, for behold your reward is great in heaven." Luke vi. 22, 23. Accordingly we find the apostles rejoiced that they were counted worthy to suffer shame for his name's sake. Therefore, says Paul, I take pleasure in infirmities, in reproaches, in necessities, in distresses, for Christ's sake; for when I am weak, then am I strong. 2 Cor. xii. 10.

Wherefore let no man's heart fail him because

of these things, nor be discouraged because of the way: the Lord is able to make you rejoice in tribulation, through which you must enter the kingdom, and at last will crown your conflicts with victory, and turn your pensive sighs into perpetual songs. Keep in view the blessed Jesus as your pattern, who, when he was reviled, reviled not again. Return not railing for railings, but pity and pray for them who despitefully use you and persecute you, saying, Father, forgive them, for they know not what they do. Take care that you are neither ashamed of religion, nor a shame to it; but in all things be circumspect, considering him that endured such contradiction of sinners against himself, lest ye be wearied and faint in your minds. As he through the hope set before him endured the cross, and despised the shame, therefore arm yourself likewise with the same mind; and having put on the whole armor of God, stand fast in the faith, quit yourselves like men, be strong in the name of the Lord, lift up your banners, and fight the good fight of faith. The heroic Paul, when he reconnoitered the host of inveterate foes, and viewed surrounding difficulties and approaching dangers, said, "None of these things move me, neither count I my life dear unto myself, so that I might finish my course with joy;" Acts xx. 24; and when methods of prudence were proposed by his weeping friends, to avoid impending danger, he, considering the advice inconsistent with christian duty and dignity, replied with warmth and holy vehemence, "What mean ye to weep, and break mine heart? for I am ready not to be bound only, but also to die at Jerusalem for the name of the Lord Jesus." Acts xxi. 13. His heavy trials, which continued through life, he considered as light and short, when compared with the durable delights in a future world, *even a far more exceeding and eternal weight of glory.*

Then those who have faithfully followed the Lord through difficulties, dangers, and death, will meet with peculiar approbation and distinguished honors; then the Captain of our salvation shall recount his worthies; Nahum ii. 5; who will appear with the ensigns of victory and the trophies of triumph in the new Jerusalem, of whom the applauding inhabitants will with joy sing, *These are they which came out of great tribulation.* Then the trial of your faith will be found more precious than gold which perisheth. The believing Hebrews therefore took joyfully the spoiling of their goods, knowing that in heaven they had a more enduring substance; and Moses chose to suffer affliction with the people of God, esteeming the reproach of Christ greater riches than the treasures of Egypt: for he had respect unto the recompense of reward. "Behold, we count them happy who endure;" James v. 11; "for in due time ye shall reap, if ye faint not;" "therefore, my beloved brethren, be ye steadfast, unmoveable, always abounding in the work of the Lord, forasmuch as ye know that your labor is not in vain in the Lord." 1 Cor. xv. 58.

CHAPTER III.

ERRORS OF FALSE RELIGIONISTS.

SOME are prevented attending to practical religion, by being told that believers are not in any sense under the law.

By the law we are frequently to understand the covenant of works, or that compact and agreement which God made with Adam, as the public head and representative of his offspring. Adam was under a natural and necessary obligation to obey his Maker's will, and was absolutely dependent on God's sovereign pleasure for the continuance of his happy existence. A right to everlasting life he could never have procured by his most ardent affection and strict obedience to God and his law; the Lord therefore kindly connected the promise of life with man's natural duty, and threatened death in case of failure. Thus Adam's motives to obedience were increased, being made a trustee for his numerous descendants.

In that covenant a small and easy test of his subjection to God was fixed upon. Nothing more than a prohibition of one tree, while the vast and various productions in the garden of God were liberally granted for his pleasure and profit. In the midst of it likewise, flourished that which was an emblem and pledge of the promised blessing, called *The Tree of Life*, which would serve to confirm his faith in his covenant God, and invigorate his hope, that his obedience might be secured, in order to the enjoyment of the gracious reward, and that he might escape the threatened punishment.

Alas! notwithstanding the said agreement was so advantageous in its nature, it was broken by our first parent, whereby all right to life, on the footing of law, was forever forfeited, according to that covenant; and death, the threatened penalty, was incurred, not only respecting his own person, but his posterity also. "Wherefore, as by one man sin entered into the world, and death by sin, so death passed upon all, for that all have sinned." Rom. v. 12. Through the offence of one many be dead, v. 15; for by one man's offence death reigned. By the offence of one, judgment came upon all men; for by one man's disobedience, many were made sinners; v. 16—19.

The apostle proves there was a covenant or law before that given by Moses, according to which the whole human race were under sentence of condemnation; for before the law (given on Mount Sinai) sin was in the world; but sin is not imputed where there is no law. Nevertheless, death reigned from Adam to Moses, even over them that had not sinned after the similitude of Adam's transgression. Rom. v. 13, 14. The law of Moses was not given that sinners might obtain life by it; for by the law is the knowledge of sin. Rom. iii. 20. It was added because of transgressions, (Gal. iii. 19,) that the offence might abound, (Rom. v. 20,) that every mouth may be stopped, and the whole world may become guilty before God; therefore by the deeds of the law, there shall no flesh be justified in his sight. Rom. iii. 19, 20.

That no man is justified by the law in the sight of God is evident; for the just shall live by faith, and the law is not of faith, but the man that doth them shall live in them. Gal. iii. 11, 12. Whosoever shall keep the whole law, and yet offend in one point, he is guilty of all. James ii. 10; for, considering the law as a covenant, sin destroys a title to legal life, and exposes the guilty to its awful penalty: for as many as are of the works of the law, are under the curse; for it is written, cursed is every one that continueth not in all things which are written in the book of the law to do them. Gal. iii. 10; Deut. xxvii. 26.

Believers, therefore, are not under the law as a covenant; their right to eternal life, does not arise from personal obedience, nor is their hope of freedom from punishment founded on any compensation which they have made or can make for their crimes. Through Christ they are dead to the law as promising life, or threatening death; they are neither under its promise nor its penalty; their covenant connexion with the law is dissolved, and a marriage to Christ commenced, that they might bring forth fruit unto God. See Rom. vii. 1 to 7. That real believers *are not under the law, but under grace,* is an undeniable truth. But it is equally evident, *they are not without law to God, but are under the law to Christ.* That there is no contradiction in these scriptural propositions will appear, if we consider the following things:

1. That by the term *law,* we are to understand the rule of moral and positive obedience. Moral obedience ariseth from our natural connexion with God as the Author of our existence and with our fellow creatures, and consisteth in supreme love to God, and an equal love to our neighbor as to ourselves; so that the whole is comprehended in love. Moral commands are founded on the natural fitness of things, and, therefore, are binding on all rational creatures. While the relation continues between the Creator and his creatures, their obligation to love him as their chief good, and to live to his honor as their ultimate end, can never cease; therefore, the law, by which such love and obedience are enforced,

cannot possibly vary. Jehovah does not demand our love because of his authority over us, but because of his own excellency, and his relation to us. He does not become the only proper object of our supreme love because he hath commanded us so to love him, but because he is the only *fit* object. The moral law does not *make* any duty proper, but declares and requires what *is* so. Moral commands, therefore, differ from,

2. Positive appointments; which arise simply from the will of God, and are, therefore, alterable in their nature, being altogether dependant on his pleasure and sovereign determination. The propriety of moral obedience, the light of nature or right reason may discover; but no idea can be formed of positive obedience, except in consequence of Divine revelation. The former is due from every creature, whether angelic or human: the subjects of the latter are particularly described in the holy Scriptures.

Thus the whole code of ceremonial law was confined to Israel, as a shadow of good things to come, and was done away in Christ, who was the substance which these laws tended to exhibit, and the end in which they terminated. But the moral law ever was, and ever will be, equally binding on all: it being the rule of that love and obedience which Jews and Gentiles own to Jehovah, the supreme good and fountain of existence; and to each other, considered as his offspring.

Notwithstanding the ceremonial law under the Old Testament was accomplished in Christ, and done away by his death, he then, as it were, nailing it to his cross, yet many Jews who believed in Jesus continued much attached to the shadow, though the substance was come. The apostles, therefore, labored to prove the abrogation of that law by which those ceremonial observances became binding on the people of God, in the former dispensation. These appointments had been justly revered and esteemed, and were to Israel very beneficial to humble them under a sense of pollution and guilt, and liability to punishment, and to direct their faith and hope to the promised Messiah.

The law was, therefore, to them a schoolmaster under Christ. But after Christ was come, they were no longer under a schoolmaster. Gal. iii. 24, 25. Those painful and tedious appointments becoming unprofitable, the great apostle labored to convince these judaizing believers, that they were not under that law. Gal. iii. 21. With great difficulty were the Jews brought off from ceremonial observances; therefore, those inspired penmen, in speaking of the church of Christ as delivered from the law, and those tedious, painful, and *now* unprofitable appointments, which were abrogated, make use of the most contemptuous terms; calling them beggarly elements, carnal ordinances, &c.

But the duties of the moral law are enforced by the strongest motives. In that law Paul delighted after the inner man; and the charge of making it *void* through the faith of the gospel he denies with holy vehemence, and indignation. Do we then make void the law through faith? God forbid. Yea, we establish the law. Rom. iii. 31.*

3. From the universal extent of the moral law, the apostle proves that Gentiles as well as Jews were under sin, and therefore exposed to punishment; that a title to life could not arise out of human obedience, because, according to the rule of righteousness, every one is culpable. Being condemned for dispositions and acts contrary to law, consequently by the deeds of the law no flesh living could be justified. A believer's title to life, and exemption from punishment, springs from another source. Therefore, such are said not to be under the law, but under the administration of grace; for the law is the ministration of death to every transgressor, and by it indignation and wrath,

* See a sermon by the Rev. Caleb Evans, entitled, The Law established by the Gospel; Dr. Gill on the Law in the Hand of Christ; and the Death of Legal Hope the life of evangelical obedience: by Rev. Abraham Booth.

tribulation and anguish are denounced against every soul of man that doth evil, of the Jew first, and also of the Gentile.

Immanuel having fulfilled its precepts and endured its penalty in favor of his people, has delivered them from deserved punishment, and given them a right to life, founded on his infinite merits. Believers are therefore delivered from the law as a covenant. From it life is not expected by them, nor by it death inflicted upon them, because they are not under the law, but under the influences, promises, and blessings of grace. Yet they do not, they cannot from thence infer, that their obligation to love and obey God is by this diminished, but on the contrary, infinitely increased.

If any, professing godliness, deny the law of the Lord to be the rule of obedience, charity obliges us to hope their meaning is injudiciously expressed; for some people's *words* and *ideas* differ so much, that a reconciliation is scarcely expected. But those who deliberately maintain that *believers are not under the law as a rule of life*, and act on such a principle, give full evidence that they are grossly ignorant of (not to say at enmity with) the nature of God, his government, and gospel.

A more pernicious sentiment, or a greater absurdity, was never invented, than this Antinomian tenet. It tends to destroy every idea of good and evil, of right and wrong, by denying the existence or use of that by which the nature of thoughts and actions is tried. It renders believers incapable of sorrowing for sin, as done either by themselves or other christians. For where there is no law, there is no transgression. It makes penitence an infallible mark of impiety, and delight in the law of God a delusion; it tends to prevent a believer from praying for Divine direction; because, however he wander, he is never wrong, nor ever in danger of stepping aside out of the path of duty, being not obliged to walk in any. A believer must not pray to be kept from evil; lest it grieve him, for sin he cannot, do what he may, sin being a transgression of the law. Nor can he ask God to forgive him any debt, being confident that he does not owe his Lord one farthing. Whatever may have been the case heretofore, he being now a lawless person, no demand can be made upon him!

In a word, Antinomianism teaches a believer neither to fear God nor to regard man; for, according to it, he cannot be guilty of offending the one nor of injuring the other; for as there is no law, cruelty is not prohibited, nor kindness required; but truth and treachery, profanity and piety, love and hatred, are equally agreeable in believers.

But brethren, ye have not so learned Christ, if so be that ye have heard him, and been taught of him as the truth is in Jesus. Eph. iv. 20, 21. You will not only rejoice in your relation to the Lord, but each believer ought to consider himself as under infinite obligation to love him, to obey him, and to adhere to him, becoming the nature of his connexions with him, even as a subject to a sovereign,—1 Thess. ii. 12; Col. i. 10–13,—a spouse to her husband,—Eph. v. 23, 29,—a soldier to his general,—2 Tim. ii. 3,—a servant to his master,—1 Pet. ii. 16; Rom. vi. 16–22,—and a child to a tender compassionate parent, Eph. v. 1. We beseech you, brethren, and exhort you by the Lord Jesus, that as ye have received of us how you ought to walk, and to please God, so ye will abound more and more, 1 Thess. iv. 1; knowing that the law is good, if a man use it lawfully. 1 Tim. i. 8. "For this is a faithful saying, That they who have believed in God should be careful to maintain good works. These things are good and profitable to men." "And let every one that nameth the name of Christ depart from iniquity."

Nothing is more evident than that believers are not under the covenant of works, but under grace. But what then? Shall we sin because we are not under the law, but under grace? God forbid! Rom. vi. 15.

Secondly. Some are stumbled in respect of the Lord's positive appointments; partly through the neglects of some, and the contemptuous manner in which others treat the ordinances of the gospel, who are notwithstanding had in reputation for religion.

Young christians are commonly much influenced by those for whom they have a veneration. Therefore, when they observe such living in the neglect of gospel ordinances, they are ready to conclude, that for them to take the lead of such eminent christians would have the appearance of pride and presumption. They therefore, through false modesty, or real fear, keep back from telling what God has done for their souls, and making a visible profession of Christ in his solemn appointments. By delays, their zeal for Christ and the love of their espousals are greatly abated, and then objections in abundance arise against its being their particular duty, on account of not having such a lively frame of mind as is thought necessary for such solemn proceedings. Thus, through their neglects, others are discouraged and prevented bearing a testimony for Jesus, as he has directed those that love him should.

For the *relief, direction*, and *animation* of such discouraged believers, I would propose to their serious consideration the following things:

1. The kindness of Christ in abolishing the vast number of ceremonial observances which were

binding under the Mosaic dispensation, and which were to Israel difficult, painful, and very expensive, called therefore a yoke of bondage. As he has appointed only two positive ordinances to be observed by his followers under the gospel, viz. Baptism and the Lord's Supper, how ungrateful is it to refuse compliance with what is so mild, so merciful, when compared with what he made the indispensable duty of those whose privileges were inexpressibly inferior to yours!

2. Though inquiring christians ought to regard the conduct of others, and are directed to go by the footsteps of the flock, and to be followers of them, who through faith and patience inherit the promises, yet none are to be imitated further than they are followers of Christ, however eminent they appear to be. The more eminent a man is for piety and talents, the more pernicious is his example when he is remiss in, or forsakes the path of duty. Perhaps some would have remonstrated against the detestable contrivance to change Jehovah's glory into the similitude of an ox, had not Aaron, the saint of God, and priest of the Most High, entered deeply into the design. But as things were, the people acquiesced with pleasure. Had their elation been a sure sign of God's approbation, all would have been well; for the congregation had "a very comfortable time," a

"delightful opportunity," till they were interrupted by Moses, who, though naturally weak, yet rebuked the transgressors with pungent severity.

Therefore call no man master on earth, relating to sacred things. It is the example and authority of Christ, your Master in heaven, who is Zion's king, which you are conscientiously to regard. You ought to love and respect all that love Jesus, but at the same time consider you *serve the Lord Christ.* And it is to your own Master you stand or fall. To him only are you accountable. None can prove they have a dispensation granted under his hand for the neglect or changing of any of his appointments; and indeed none do plead for the power of granting indulgences in his name, save the man of sin, and those delegated by him. But even supposing others to have obtained such a dispensation, what proof can be given that *you* are included in the grant? Stand not, therefore, O believer, waiting to see what this or the other good man may resolve to do, nor perplex your mind about Christ's conduct to them. Think of Christ's reply to Peter when he was so inquisitive about his brother John, saying, *Lord, what shall this man do?* How keen, and yet how kind, was the Redeemer's answer to the impertinent querist! WHAT IS THAT TO THEE? FOLLOW THOU ME. John xxi. 22.

The Divine authority is not to be trifled with. Two sons of Aaron were struck dead for daring to deviate from the Lord's command. And Moses, the man of God, had like to have lost his life through his postponing a matter of duty, probably in compliance with the solicitations of his spouse.

Perhaps you may be told by some, that an attendance to such appointments is unnecessary, as they are not saving ordinances. It might not be amiss to inquire of such people, What *are saving ordinances*? Where are they to be found? If none are saving, then, according to the objection, none ought to be attended to. No works of righteousness should be performed; because salvation is not of works, but of grace. It is astonishing that such a mongrel maxim should ever be used by those who abhor *Antinomian liberty*, and *Arminian legality*, seeing the nature of both are therein united! It is the genuine offspring of those two very opposite and equally absurd sentiments. Has Jesus in very deed lost all his authority, that his appointments should sink into insignificancy? and has Christ done so little for his people, that they are under no manner of obligation, out of gratitude, to act for him? Has the love of Jesus lost its constraining influence? And ought christians to be realy indifferent about serving God any further than they can merit by it?

Is the dying request of dear friends usually regarded by the surviving relatives, and shall not our best friend, our dying Immanuel, be listened to with cordial affection, when he appointed the ordinance of the Supper, saying, "This do in remembrance of me?" Afterwards he sent from heaven, by the apostle Paul, a renewal of his request to the churches. See 1 Cor. xi. His ordinances are his palaces where he shows his glory, and feasts with his people, saying, "Eat, O friends, drink, yea, drink abundantly, O beloved." Come forward, then, ye friends of Jesus, follow his example, and receive the kind memorials of his love.

Thirdly. Divine acquirements being superior to the ability of men in their present fallen condition, have been exceedingly perplexing to many; especially such as feel themselves without strength, which the Scriptures declare them to be for whom Christ died, and to whom he says, without me ye can do nothing, John xv. 5, whose experience of their utter inability and absolute dependence on the Lord coincides with what the apostle expresses concerning himself and his brethren, who were even able ministers of the New Testament. Their language is, who is sufficient for these things? 2 Cor. ii. 16.

We are not sufficient of ourselves, but our

sufficiency is of God. 2 Cor. iii. 5. From a consciousness of personal inability, joined with a conviction of absolute and necessary obligation to obedience, arise various difficulties relating to the *equity* of God in requiring that of his creatures which he knows and declares it is not in their power to perform. To maintain that men have an inherent power to turn to God and embrace the gospel, and glorify him in a course of holy obedience, *without* the infusion of supernatural principles, is to oppose the positive declarations of God's word respecting the necessity of regeneration, and the impossibility of those who are in the flesh doing anything pleasing and acceptable to God. See Rom. viii. 5, 8.

Those who oppose the doctrine of free grace are constrained to plead for the power of man to love and obey God, representing men's inability as absolutely inconsistent with Scriptural commands and exhortations to obedience and faith. These declaim with an air of triumph on the absurdity of supposing God to require impossibilities; in which those heartily concur who represent men as quite blameless, though disobedient, because they have no power of themselves to obey.

Various methods have been taken to apologize for man's imperfections, and extenuate his guilt. As men are naturally disaffected to God, it is no wonder they should endeavor to new model his government according to their different inclinations, in order to keep conscience easy, and support a pleasing expectation of future happiness without holiness; or being beholden to his clemency and grace. Every opposition to the gospel, every false scheme of divinity, agree in supposing the law of God too severe; and that it ought to be, if possible, accommodated to men's present condition; though they greatly differ as to how it may be accomplished. Those who think the law of God cannot be altered or explained so as to suit the carnal mind, and having an equal aversion to internal purity as to the law which requires it, plead for an exemption from its hateful authority, esteeming it a peculiar privilege to settle if possible in the province of Antinomianism; a state so far from God, that the wretched inhabitants suppose his dominion does not extend to them.

All false systems unite in proof of one important truth, which is, that till God's law be approved as just in all its demands and denunciations, the gospel will never be properly understood and cordially embraced; which the following brief remarks may sufficiently evince, as well as prepare the way to a solution of the difficulty in question.

1. Some confidently assert that on the failure of man in his obedience, the perfections of God

obliged him to *alter* the constitution of his government so far, as that there was no need at all of Christ's death to procure an exemption from punishment. That *repentance* and *pardon* are connected by the law of natural *equity*. That Christ came not to make a reconciliation for iniquity, but only as a pattern of acceptable obedience, and to confirm his doctrine by sealing it with his blood. But, in confirmation of the truth for which he was condemned, Christ could have prayed to his Father, who would have sent more than twelve legions of angels to have delivered him from death. But how then (said he) should the Scriptures be fulfilled, that thus it must be, (Matt. xxvi. 53, 54,) for without shedding of blood there is no remission. Heb. ix. 22.

Admitting that Christ came only as an example, will it not follow that the law which he came to obey required purity of nature and perfect obedience; seeing our pattern was the subject of both? If the law did not require perfect obedience, but *repentance* was substituted and accepted in its stead, and Christ came to set *us* an example *how* we might obtain salvation; is it not natural to infer, that in order to his being a proper pattern to us for *such* a purpose and end, he should have been *deficient* in his obedience, and the subject of *sincere repentance?* and *thus* have demonstrated for our encouragement and imitation, that though he was *imperfect* as we are, yet by being *penitent,* he obtained the forgiveness of all his imperfections.

This scheme, it must be acknowledged, so far as relates to *acceptance* with God, entirely excludes the necessity of Christ; he being neither a proper *pattern* to show *how* they might obtain salvation, nor its *procuring* author. However, by such a rejection of Jesus the Scriptures are fulfilled, which say, if there had been a law which could have given life, verily righteousness had been by the law. Gal. iii. 21. And if righteousness came by the law, then Christ is dead in vain. Gal. ii. 21. If the death of Christ was entirely in vain, his laying down his life, when there was no need for it, cannot be deemed an example *worthy* of our imitation; for no man, however heroic, has a right to throw away his life to no purpose. So far from its being virtuous, such conduct would not only be imprudent, but extremely sinful.

Can we suppose Christ came into our world on a *needless* errand, and shed his blood in *vain?* Yet shocking as the supposition is, it must be an established fact, *if* there was any law existing which could have given life. For nothing could be more evident, than that if men could have answered the demands of the law, there would have been no need of the obedience and death of Jesus, according to the reasoning of the great apostle. This system, therefore, tends to *embarrass,* instead of solving the question, respecting the *equity* of God in requiring that of his creatures which they are now unable to perform.

2. Some suppose the difficulty would be removed if it might be allowed that Christ by his death procured or engaged the Father's love to sinners, so far as to obtain a *relaxation* of that law under which they originally were, and establish a milder system of government suited to the condition of his rebellious subjects. But this plea is quite inadmissible, because the love of God, from which salvation springs, was the *cause* of Christ's coming to die for transgressors. "God so loved the world, that he gave his only begotten Son." John iii. 16. "In this was manifested the love of God towards us, that God sent his Son into the world, that we might live through him." John iv. 9. "Hereby we perceive the love of God, because he laid down his life for us." Chap. iii. 16.

Christ did not procure a new remedial law, because that *law* under which sinners *are,* requires perfect obedience, on pain of perpetual punishment. "Cursed is every one that continueth not in all things written in the book of the law to do them, and as many as are of the works of the law are under its curse." Gal. iii. 10. The law under which sinners *are*, is that according to which the world stands condemned as criminal at Jehovah's bar, and by the deeds of which no flesh shall be justified in his sight. Rom. iii. 19, 20.

Those who think a relaxation of the law is obtained, ought to point out wherein the *abatement* consisteth, that men might keep in a happy medium, and not presume to go *beyond* nor *fall short* in obedience to its precepts. Will the Lord allow men to have other gods besides himself, or to worship him in a way contrary to what he has appointed? Will he hold them guiltless that take his name is vain? May people now lawfully forget to keep holy the Sabbath day? Has Christ released men from their natural obligations to parents? or given them a license to murder, to live in uncleanness, or falsely to accuse their neighbours, or covet what is the property of others? If moral commands continue in full force, as is abundantly evident from the New Testament, wherein then does the alteration consist? Does the law cease to take cognizance of the heart, and being *less spiritual* is it, therefore, *more agreeable* to the carnal mind? If that be the case, how can *mental* acts be condemned by it, which the Scriptures *positively* declare they are? Impure desires are by it deemed adultery; hatred, murder; and covetousness, idolatry. See Matt. v. 28; 2 Pet. ii. 14; 1 John iii. 15; Col. iii. 5. The language of christians in the apostolic day was, we know the law is spiritual. Rom. vii. 14. It is holy, just and good. Rom. vii. 12. I delight in it after the inward man, says Paul, verse 22, so then with my mind I serve the law of God, verse 25.

The law of which the apostle spoke, and in which he delighted was that which slew him, that commandment which was ordained to life, he (as a criminal,) found to be unto death, verse 10, 11. He was delivered from it as a covenant, but under it as an unalterable law, verse 6, 7. As a covenant it was weak, (that it could not give life to the sinner,) not weak in its own nature, much less wicked, but weak through the flesh. What it could not, therefore, do in favor of the guilty, was done by Jesus, who did not blame the law, but justified and satisfied its demands, and condemned all opposition to it, even *sin in the flesh.* Rom. viii. 3. The law under which christians are, requires truth in the inward parts as much as ever, and cannot alter whilst Jehovah remains the same: for God is a Spirit, and they that worship him MUST worship him in spirit and in truth. John iv. 24.

If then both the *matter* and spiritual nature of moral obedience remain the same, notwithstanding men's inability, it is evident the law by which obedience is enforced is not *altered*, and that a new remedial law is a *fiction*. Besides, if the law became unrighteous when its subjects became ungodly, (which would be blasphemy to suppose,) God would certainly have repealed it, and not sent his son to honor an unjust law, at the expense of his blood.

Finally. If the Divine law ceaseth to require perfect obedience, saints will at last rise in obedience superior to the law under which they are; for *the spirits of just men will be made perfect*, and when so they will love God more than he 'desires they should, unless the law *rise* and *fall* in its requirements according to the *inclination* of its subjects, on which absurd hypothesis the notion of a *new* law seems to be founded.

The gospel exhibits new *motives* to love and obedience, and graciously conveys new *principles*, in consequence of which saints yield to God *new obedience*, and by his authority attend to *new positive ordinances*, for new and special purposes; and are accepted of God, and approach him under *new characters*, in a *new and living way;* and are encouraged by *new* and *better* promises, in consequence of the new and well ordered covenant of grace, under which they are. But though he make *all things new* in respect of *acceptance* with him, and *enjoyment* of him and old things pass away in favor of them who inhabit the *new Jerusalem*, yet as God is the same, without variableness, in his own adorable perfections, infinite beauty, and boundless authority, he cannot alter his moral law, considered *simply* as a law, because *moral* obligations arise from that *natural* connexion and relation subsisting between God and rational creatures, considered as the productions of his power. Hence it is that no alteration in them can possibly diminish their obligations to him.

It is no new thing for professors of religion to show an inclination to excuse themselves, and throw the blame upon God. A certain wicked and slothful servant, when called to an account by his master, could say, "Lord, I knew thee to be an hard man, reaping where thou hast not sown, and gathering where thou hast not strewed, and I was afraid, and went and hid my Lord's money." Matt. xxv. 24. Sinners in general think their cases would not be so extremely bad as the Scriptures assert and they frequently fear, were they *fairly* dealt with. Instead of taking blame and shame to themselves, their powers are employed to find out other methods to appease conscience, and support hope, than that which is set before them in the gospel.

3. Some apprehend the difficulty may be solved by supposing a certain degree of grace bestowed on all men, in order to enable them to perform what

is necessary to the enjoyment of God's friendship and favor. But the difficulty is rather increased than diminished by this contrivance. For,

If such degrees of grace be necessary to enable men to obey, and to render their disobedience *inexcusable,* it necessarily supposes, that unless such a degree of what is called *common grace* was given them of God, they could not have been judged blamable for the want of obedience. If they were not blamable before, or antecedent to the supposed grace being bestowed, they certainly were not liable to punishment. And if not liable to punishment *before* they had this common grace conferred on them, how is this common grace an advantage? seeing that without it they were safe, but the possession of it has rendered their state at best precarious!

Again; if such grace be given not so much for *their advantage,* as to *vindicate Jehovah's character,* which is by some supposed to be the design of it, it is necessarily implied, that *without* such a bestowment, his conduct would have been liable to censure and impeachment, and not at all capable of being defended as equitable and just.

Further. If without the bestowment of the aforesaid grace, men would have had cause to complain of *unfair* dealing, what is called common grace is, in fact, no other than a *common debt,* which God could not justly withhold from any man. Thus the doctrine of common grace represents the Lord as neither generous nor just. It is the same as saying, If God will please to do us justice, we will out of complaisance call it *grace*. But, as a proof of esteeming what we call grace a proper *debt*, and no real *favor*, we, in our hearts, verily account, and are bold to declare that without such a bestowment, we should have had cause for ever to *complain* of *harsh* treatment.

Thus it appears that all erroneous systems, however widely they differ, agree in tacitly charging God and his law with injustice in condemning for sin; and that the enmity of carnal men is such, that they cannot be reconciled to his government, unless certain concessions be made on his part to obtain *their* forgiveness of the supposed injury. However, it is evident, that approving views of the requirements of God's law are absolutely necessary, in order to admiring views of the grace in his gospel. For where condemnation would be *unjust* an acquittal is no *favor;* and where obedience is not due, it cannot be justly demanded.

Another method of accounting for God's requiring perfect obedience of imperfect men, is the consideration of our being represented by Adam, in the covenant which was made with him.

The reasoning of many eminent men has been thus:—"We had in Adam full and adequate ability, every way proportionable to the nature and extent of duty; and though men have lost their power to obey, God has neither lost nor given up his authority to command: therefore it is our duty to exert not only the strength we are now possessed of, but likewise the strength we should have had, supposing our first parent had continued in that state of purity and power."

That Adam was the covenant head of his posterity, appears evident from the Scriptures, and I hope, has been proved under another head. And, that advantages and disadvantages naturally result from representation, according as representatives act in their public character, none will deny. The covenant made with our first parent was certainly righteous; and had the condition been performed, we should all have admired, not only the equity, but the kindness of the compact. But, success does not make a transaction equitable, nor does a failure constitute a stipulation wrong which is naturally right; and we may rest satisfied, that it was impossible for an infinitely holy God and an innocent creature to enter into an agreement essentially wrong. Therefore, we ought to be for ever silent, in respect of censure and complaint.

Though this last-mentioned method of accounting for the Lord's requiring of us what is superior to our present power be less exceptionable than those before referred to, yet it does not come fully to the point, or cast sufficient light upon the subject; for it seems contrary to the common or known rules of equity, to punish on account of not performing what is *naturally* impossible to be performed.

Hence, some have endeavored to hold up the doctrines of grace as objects of ridicule and contempt, and have boldly asserted, that according to these doctrines, future judgment would be a mere farce. For God might as justly punish slow-moving animals for deficiency in swiftness, and those for not flying who have no wings, nor in any respect formed for such a motion, as to punish men for not doing what they cannot possibly accomplish, but is as much above their power as to create a world. Such *checks* the adherents to truth have frequently met with. And such reasoning, or rather declamation, has been very stumbling to weak Christians. Some have been severely tried by the above misrepresentation of gospel truths, and tempted to think what they dare not utter.

For the relief of such, I propose to their calm and candid consideration a distinction between natural and moral inability, which seems necessary to be well understood in order to obtain consistent views of Divine revelation, relating to the requirements of God's righteous law and the nature of his precious gospel.

By *natural* inability, is intended a want of a natural capacity or opportunity to know and do what is commanded, or an absolute defect in the natural powers of a man's mind or body, by which he is rendered incapable of acting, although his will were bent upon the performance of his duty. Whatever totally prevents a person's knowing or doing any thing, though he be ever so desirous of accomplishing it, is what I wish to have considered as included in natural inability.

Moral inability consists in a disinclination to what is good, or an aversion to what God has made a duty. That I may be properly understood, I would further observe, that by natural power and ability, is intended, the possession or enjoyment of such powers and properties of soul and body, as are necessary for the purpose of mental and corporeal actions, and also being in a situation suitable for the exertion of them.

By moral ability is intended a suitable disposition, which consists in a holy inclination to what is truly good. To illustrate and point out the propriety and utility of the above distinction, for the relief of entangled minds, I shall endeavor to demonstrate, that natural inability, as above stated, is not a criminal defect; and that moral inability is inseparably connected with fault, and cannot possibly be an excuse or palliation of blame, but on the contrary, that a man is culpable, because of his inability to obey; or that criminality increases in proportion to the degree of moral impotency.

1. That *natural* inability is not a criminal defect, or culpable deficiency, will appear evident, if the following observations be duly attended to.

Though men's powers of mind and body are greatly impaired by the fall, or the entrance of sin, yet the Scriptures do not intimate that *weaknesses*, in either, are sinful; they are spoken of as pitiable infirmities, but never as punishable faults. Therefore it is written, as a father pitieth his children, so the Lord pitieth them that fear him. He considers our frame, and remembers we are but dust. Parents, by whose pity the Lord illustrates his own, know how to make this distinction respecting their children, and would be cruel if they did not. Supposing a son in the height of some criminal proceeding should break his legs, would it not be deemed cruel, not only to punish him for the criminal action by which he came by his disaster, but for his not walking, which he would be very glad to do if he could. Upon this self-evident principle of equity, Mephibosheth founded his plea, when accused by his servant of disloyalty to king David his sovereign. He loved David's person and government, and he pleaded, that his not accompanying him in a time of trouble, when he fled before his unnatural son, was not owing to *disaffection*, but "*thy servant is lame.*"

It is not the sin of the blind that they do not read the Scriptures; nor are the deaf blameable for not hearing the sound of the gospel: nor the dumb culpable on account of their not pleading for God. Nor is it the duty of any to work with their hands who have none. The reason is, because they *could* not be or do otherwise if they would. Though Paul's bodily presence was weak, and his speech contemptible, yet he did not consider himself criminal on that account; but rejoiced in his infirmities, that the power of Christ might rest upon him; but he did not rejoice in his sins.

Deficiency or weakness in mental powers is not criminal; for in that case, the weakest man would be the most wicked, and those who are superior in natural parts would always excel in piety; which is contrary to fact. Men are dead in sin, but that death does not consist in a privation of *natural* faculties. When rationality is absent, words and actions are never deemed punishable, because they are not accounted criminal. But if the fault lay in *natural* weakness, the less understanding and reason a person is possessed of at any time, the greater would be his crimes. And instead of not being punished for injuring others, such ought to be punished with greater severity on that account.

In regeneration the Holy Spirit does not create new *faculties*, or bestow a new set of natural powers; he does not produce a new head, but a new heart, by infusing new principles and holy dispositions. But if a deficiency in *natural* powers was the fountain of fault, or the source of blame, from whence criminal actions proceed, there would be a necessity for the production of new faculties, or otherwise a removal of their natural deficiencies. And if so, the surest evidences of a gracious change would be a strong memory, a fertile imagination, a fund of wit, a profound understanding, clear ideas, and strong reasoning. In short, an assemblage of fine brilliant parts would, in that case, be the best proof of true holiness. And thus the devil might perhaps be admired for his purity; for, according to that mode of reasoning, Satan might be proved a delightful saint.

No greater natural powers are necessary to love God, than to hate him; to serve him, than to oppose him. Therefore God does not require more of any man than the right use of what he hath. And surely it is not wrong to require what is right. God does not require any thing unreasonable; he requires only what he has a right to, and deserves; even all the heart, all the soul, and all the strength.

He does not require in point of degree the like of all; for to whom much is given, of them he requires the more. Luke xii. 48. It is each one's *all* that he demands; he does not require his creatures to be alike strong in mental powers: he never intended they should be. Angels excel in strength; but he requires all his rational creatures to love and serve him with all the strength they have. He could not require more with equity to his creatures, nor dispense with less in justice to himself. He requires nothing *naturally* impossible to be performed. He has not made any thing the duty of his creatures which exceeds their natural ability, nor does he punish them for not acquiring or doing what is naturally beyond their power to perform. As men's natural capacities and situations are very different, he does not, therefore, require all men to be alike knowing, nor does he require knowledge beyond the means of information. He does not condemn those who have no revelation, for not knowing what is only knowable by revelation; nor expect of those who have the Scriptures to know a tittle more than is revealed by them.

Hence, as to those things which are only revealed as matters of fact, to be ignorant *how* they are, is not the sin of any man. Though God exhorts to liberality, yet none are required to give liberally who have nothing to bestow. Duty is measured by natural ability; and where that is wanting, the Lord accepts of a *willing mind.* 2 Cor. viii. 12. Where the disposition is right, and the design or intention good, the want of ability to act as intended, exculpates the person from criminality in that respect. In a word, the good man is not blamable because he cannot do so much for God as he would; nor is the bad man commendable, because he cannot do evil according to his desire. Many wicked men would be greater villains than they are, if they knew how. But though they have not ability or opportunity to act out their inclinations, none will commend them on that account. See Acts xxiii. 12; 1 Kings viii. 18.

As commendation and blame do not result from natural ability or inability, but from dispositions and voluntary acts, therefore, Jehovah's conduct stands clear from the imputation of injustice or cruelty, seeing his requirements are proportionate to, and nothing more than a right use of the natural powers, and privileges which his creatures possess. His commands are not grievous in their own nature, whatever they be to our corrupt minds.

They are agreeable, and suited to the natural *powers* of men, however contrary and disgustful to their natural *inclinations*.

2. If we attend seriously to *moral* inability, we shall discover the awful condition in which men naturally are, and the absolute necessity of omnipotent grace to deliver them from a state evidently helpless, and deplorable. For such cannot love God, nor contribute in the least to their own deliverance; and yet their criminality is equal to their inability. A sinner while unrenewed by grace cannot love God, obey the law, or embrace the gospel, because the carnal mind is enmity against God, and is not subject to the law of God, neither indeed can be. Rom viii. 7. The wicked *will* not seek after God: God is not in all his thoughts. Psalm x. 4. Such do not *like* to retain God in their hearts; therefore *desire* not the knowledge of his ways. Rom. i. 28; Job xxi. 14. Yea, they treat him with scorn and disdain. Ps. x. 13. Being the subjects of dispositions contrary to his holy nature, they are therefore alienated from the life of God, and dead in trespasses and in sins. Eph. ii. 1; and iv. 18. The natural man is blind to the moral excellency and beauty of God; to the spiritual glories of Christ and his kingdom. He has no perception of the things of the Spirit of

God, neither can he know them, because they are spiritually discerned. 1 Cor. ii. 14.

As unconverted sinners cannot be subject to the law of God, so they cannot embrace the gospel. Jesus declared it impossible while they continue in that state, saying, "No man *can* come unto me, except the Father which hath sent me draw him." John vi. 44. "The Spirit of truth the world *cannot* receive." John xiv. 17. "Why do ye not understand my speech? Even because ye *cannot* hear my word." John viii. 43. "Their ear is uncircumcised, and they *cannot* hearken." The reason is not *natural* but *moral* inability, for "behold the word of the Lord is unto them a *reproach*, they have no *delight* in it." Jer. vi. 10. Their hearts are destitute of spiritual emotions, and compared to "stone;" even to the "adamant," which is harder than "flint." So then they that are in the flesh *cannot* please God, being under the dominion of dispositions *averse* to his nature and will. Rom. viii. 8.

They cannot love and obey God, till they are inclined so to do; and no man can be so disposed to love God, till he view him as an agreeable object. And God never was agreeable to a carnal mind, it being enmity against him, on which account it *is* not, *cannot* be subject to him.

Such will neglect and despise God, while they

continue to prefer other things before him. Those therefore who are lovers of pleasures more than lovers of God, cannot possibly esteem him as the chief good; and unless he be loved as such, he is not, as God, loved at all. Those who love the praise of men more than the praise of God, *cannot* seek the honor which cometh from him only. For every one, if not prevented, will undoubtedly pursue what he prefers, or act according to his prevailing inclinations. Those, therefore, could not believe in, or adhere to the humble Jesus, who were ambitious of human honor. To such he said, How *can* ye believe which receive honor one of another? John v. 44.

But some may ask, "May not such persons love God, repent and believe the gospel if they will?"

Answer, "Most certainly they may if they *choose* to do so." There is nothing to prevent their doing so, wherever the gospel is published, but their own criminal dispositions. There is no bar in their way, but the wickedness of their hearts. Whosoever will are invited to come and take of the waters of life freely. Rev. xxii. 17. They have faculties or powers of mind adequate to what God requires of them. It is not owing to the want of natural ability, as before stated, but their impotency consists in *aversion* to the things of God. When that is removed the difficulty is over. For, where God is loved, sin will be hated, Christ admired, and the gospel embraced, with cordial affection and faith.

But while men are in a carnal state, they cannot choose what is spiritually good; for that would suppose them capable of choosing what they do not approve of, or of preferring what they do not esteem, but to which they have a fixed aversion. While a person sees no comeliness in Christ, he cannot possibly choose him as the chief among ten thousand—his all in all; which believers do. Nor can he hate sin till it become disagreeable to him; or sincerely seek the salvation of God till he feels he wants it, and knows its worth.

The question therefore should rather be, whether any unrenewed person ever did, or can choose to love God, hate sin, and cordially embrace the gospel? For, if none while in that state or condition ever did or can, make such a choice, a *willingness* in such a case is not supposable.

If unconverted persons may love God, repent, and truly believe in Jesus, conversion would be needless so far as it relates to such well-disposed persons; for true believing penitents shall be saved. And if so, such may be in heaven who never were born again, contrary to the express and solemn declarations of the Saviour, except a man be born again, he cannot see the kingdom of God; except ye be converted and become as little children, ye shall not enter into the kingdom of heaven. John iii. 3, 5, 7; Matt. xviii. 3.

And if unregenerate persons may love God, and obey the gospel, how are we to distinguish between those who are regenerated and those who are not? If those who turn themselves, cannot be distinguished from those whose hearts are turned by the Lord, the apostle's question to christian converts, *Who maketh thee to differ?* would be quite impertinent.

We are taught by the unerring word, that there is a great likeness to, and as close a connexion between men's voluntary actions and internal principles, as between the nature of a tree and the kind of fruit it bears, or a fountain and its streams. Matt. vii. 16, 20; James iii. 11, 12. When a corrupt fountain sends forth pure streams; and thorns, brambles, and thistles, produce figs and grapes; then, and not before, may we expect a carnal man to choose spiritual things.

But it may be replied, that as man is a free agent, he has power to choose what and when he thinks proper.

That man is a free agent cannot be denied, consistently with his being accountable for his own actions. Man's free agency consisteth in a power or capacity to compare ideas and to give a preference to what appears, all things considered, to be most agreeable to himself. Perfect freedom consisteth in a man's acting agreeably to his own inclination, without any compulsion or restraint. A man, therefore, being a free agent, will act agreeably to his own mind; therefore free agency is a farther confirmation of man's moral inability. For, as Divine things are, in their very nature, disagreeable to the unrenewed sinner; therefore, as a free agent he will, and cannot but choose the contrary, as being agreeable to the desires and bent of his soul.

It is said, "Man has a determining power over his own will, and, therefore, his will acts as he directs it, and consequently he is capable of making a commendable and virtuous choice:" this is the last resort of most sensible Armenians.

It does not seem very intelligible to talk of a power over a power, resolving to resolve, or directing that by which a man is guided, and leading what he follows. However, granting all that can be desired, man's moral inability remains just as before stated. For supposing a man to direct his will what to choose, he is sure to direct it to choose that which he thinks is best, or what is most agreeable to himself. The choice, therefore, which he is supposed to direct his will to make, cannot possibly be in favor of true religion, while spiritual things are disagreeable to him; which they will continue to be as long as his heart is unrenewed by grace.

The first supposed act of his mind, by which the subsequent act of his will is directed, must be according to the light in which he views the objects to be chosen; and while he does not view the glory and superlative excellence of Divine things, he cannot give a preference to them; for that would be preferring what he disesteems. And till he prefers them, he cannot order his will to choose them.

Thus it appears that every wicked man is held by the cords of his sins. Prov. v. 22. He feedeth on ashes; a deceived heart hath turned him aside, that he *cannot* deliver his soul, nor say, is there not a lie in my right hand? Isa. xliv. 20. That this awful state of moral inability and death, is a blameable condition, or a criminal defect, will appear from the following observations:

1. It is voluntary and free. Men are not compelled to sin contrary to their inclinations; but the hearts of the sons of men are set in them to do evil. Eccles. viii. 11. Their language is, "we have loved strangers, and after them will we go." "As for the word thou hast spoken to us from the Lord, we *will* not hearken unto thee." "Israel *would* have none of me." Ps. lxxxi. 11. "I called, but they gave me no answer; all the day long have I

stretched out my hand to a disobedient and gainsaying people, (Rom. x. 21,) "which walk in a way that was not good, after their own *thoughts*," (Isa. lxv. 2,) which say unto God, depart from us; and what can the Almighty do for them? Depart from us, for we *desire* not the knowledge of thy ways. What is the Almighty that we should serve him; and what profit should we have if we pray unto him? Job xxii. 17; chap. xxi. 11. 14. "We *will* not have this man to reign over us." The result of their consultation against the Lord, and his anointed, is, "Let us break their bands asunder and cast away their cords from us." Psa. ii. 3.

Now if men are accountable for any of their actions, they must be so for those which are voluntary. *Involuntary* acts are not criminal; they do not discover a bad disposition. A good man (like Peter) may be bound by violent hands, and carried whither he would not. In that case it is not his *fault*, though he be found in company with men of the most abandoned characters, being there contrary to his choice or inclination. A gracious person may be delirious, or in convulsions, and when so, may injure himself or his friends; as such frequently discover the greatest antipathy to those whom they most highly esteemed when in their right minds. Yet such actions are never deemed *criminal*, because they are not considered as effects of a bad disposition, but as proceeding from disorders in the animal frame. Acts of a nature much less violent and injurious, are accounted punishable when there is evidence they are entirely *voluntary* and free, or arise from a bad design.

Involuntary actions may occasion much grief when reflected upon; but a person cannot be said to repent of them, any more than a man can repent because he has not a proper perspiration or a regular pulse. Praise and blame, rewards and punishments, are only connected with those actions which are the fruit of volition. Therefore no man will be punished further than he is sinful, and no action can be deemed sinful which is not the effect of choice.

Nor is any man praiseworthy, whatever good may result to others, from his conduct, if it appears that what he did was the effect of compulsion, or with an ill design. Mordecai was not under any real obligation to Haman, though he was by him arrayed in royal apparel, and brought through the city on horseback, who likewise proclaimed before him, "*Thus shall it be done unto the man whom the king delighteth to honor!*" because what he did was contrary to his inclination or choice, being compelled through fear of the king's displeasure. Nor were Joseph's brethren commendable, though they were instruments of his advancement in Egypt; because, though they sent him thither, they meant it for evil. The devil's testimony in favor of Christ's filial relation to God did not entitle him to commendation as Peter's did, though equally true, full, and explicit, because Peter's confession was voluntary, and his intention good. He meant thereby to honor his Lord; but Satan's acknowledgment was either the effect of constraint, or done with a design to sink the Saviour's reputation. Luke iv. 41.

Hence it appears, that the criminal conduct of creatures is the effect of their choice; sinful actions are voluntary and free. Therefore no man will be found more sinful than he chose to be; and if any actions are punishable or commendable, it must be those which were voluntary; and consequently the strength of a propensity to evil, or a moral inability to do good, cannot be pleaded in favor of sinners, or as an extenuation of guilt.

2. Every apology in favor of delinquents, founded on moral inability, is not only absolutely inadmissible, according to every rule of equity, but has a direct tendency to confirm the charge of culpability, and to rivet the fetters of guilt. Men are naturally disposed to cover their transgressions, as Adam; and fix the charge of blame

elsewhere; and through confounding or blending the idea of what is *moral*, with what is *natural*, they endeavour to keep their consciences easy in sin, from such-like excuses as the following:

"If men's propensity to evil be such as that they cannot love and obey God without being created anew in Christ Jesus, they are rather the objects of pity than of blame; therefore we ought not to be condemned for what we cannot help."

To make this soothing inference consistent, these words ought to be added; i. e. *if we would.* Then it would be a good plea in favor of involuntary actions, or *natural inability;* for none are condemned for not doing what they could not possibly perform *if they would.* But as it respects moral inability, it is just the reverse; for the prevalency of inclination, or strength of propensity to good or evil, is the very thing from whence degrees in each proceed, and are inferred.

Moral evil is that which God naturally and necessarily hates, and voluntarily abhors. His propensity to purity is infinite and invariable. He therefore takes no pleasure in our obedience to his own appointments when performed in a sinful manner; he said to backslidden Israel, "Incense is an abomination to me; the new moons and sabbaths, the calling of assemblies, I cannot away with; it is iniquity, even the solemn meeting;

your new moons and your appointed feasts my soul hateth; they are a trouble to me, I am weary to bear them." Isa. i. 13, 14.

No man of common sense will infer that, because Jehovah has an infinite propensity to purity, and *cannot* but hate sin, therefore he is not glorious in holiness; or that because he cannot lie, cannot deny himself, therefore there is no need to praise *his truth*. Who, then, with the least regard to, or possessing any share of reason, truth, and decency, can thus plead, *I am not very bad, because I have a very great and constant aversion to what is good.*

If an intense love to sin, and hatred to holiness, constitute freedom from blame; those who are the greatest enemies to God and all righteousness, or most evidently belong to the children of the devil, are the least liable to punishment.

If disinclination to duty frees a person from obligation to obedience, a slothful servant would have an unanswerable argument in favor of his conduct; for he might say, (and no doubt could give a sufficient proof if necessary,) that he never *loved* work in his life, that he always had an *aversion* to hard labor, and cannot yet be reconciled to it, being contrary to his inclination; and that to which he always found, as far as he can remember, an inward fixed reluctance. He might add, Sir, when I find work *agreeable* to me, I will attend to it: but till then, you cannot be so unreasonable as to blame me, seeing we are taught to consider that, even in matters of religion, nothing is duty further than there is a corresponding disposition. I love to look on, whilst others labor, and I hope you will allow me, without offence, to act according to my natural inclination. The haughty servant might likewise say, You will allow me, I hope sir, to do as I please, for I never did love control; I was always of an ambitious temper, and have even now a strong inclination and intense desire after honor and authority. I wish you would, and therefore I cannot but hope you will, consider yourself, in future, as under my direction.

Must the notorious thief be acquitted, because he has been long under the power of a strong inclination to injure his neighbors? or the murderer be deemed less guilty, because of his cruel disposition? Were such a principle allowed, moral government would be overturned; every one might do as he pleases without liability to punishment, especially those of the *vilest* dispositions. And if so, perhaps none would deserve less punishment than the devil.

But it may be said, "Our aversion to God has been transmitted to us from our first parents; and being born so, therefore we hope favor will be shown, as our personal guilt is thereby diminished."

Were pity pleaded for, on account of natural inability, or a natural defect and affliction, attending either our mental or bodily powers, the reasonableness of the plea would readily be granted. But sin is a *moral* defect, and cannot be committed contrary to consent, or without a criminal inclination. The above extenuating plea is only a false gloss. It is as if a person should say, when indicted for high treason, "I am, it is true, a traitor, but I hope it will be considered as an extenuation of my crime, that I am the offspring and seed of evil doers; my family in all their respective generations have been rebels against their sovereign. I have, therefore, only acted as have my progenitors. I hope I shall be favorably dealt with, as my disloyalty is a family disposition. Besides, what I have done, arose from a rooted enmity in my heart to the government; for which I ought not to be censured, as my ancestors always discovered, as I have done, an inclination to overturn the constitution; and if possible to *dethrone* the sovereign, and bring him and all his children and subjects into perpetual contempt. Moreover, as my temper and disposition are such, I *cannot* submit to his authority, nor be beholden to *his* clemency; having a rivetted aversion in my heart to what he is, has, does, and says. If, therefore, my own enmity, or my father's, against the sovereign and his subjects have any influence to exculpate or diminish the charge of guilt, which doubtless ought to be allowed in my favor, I hope, according to the law of equity, my punishment (if any be justly inflicted) will be very small."

If it would be an affront to common sense, and contrary to every rule of equity amongst men, to plead an exemption from punishment, on account of the delinquent's vile disposition, or that of his ancestors, how awful then is the deception of those who apprehend that they cannot be treated as criminals, because of moral inability, or the badness of their hearts.

Besides, if the vileness of men's hearts, or their abominable dispositions, free them from blame, or secure them from punishment, they cannot account them to be bad hearts, seeing their present peace and future hope depend upon them. They are not, it seems, injurious hearts, but extremely beneficial, providing they be but *sufficiently* vile. Such persons would not know how to go on in religion as they do—they could not sin without sorrow, hope without holiness, believe without evidence, and rejoice in a thing of nought; but through the help of a bad heart. They do not think them deceitful above all things, and desperately wicked, and that for the badness of them they are accountable to God. They consider their base hearts, and vile dispositions, as their best friends, which justify and sanctify their omissions of duty, and commission of sins.

The gospel libertine, yea, the whole tribe of indolent, light, and trifling professors, seem to consider and use what they call their bad heart, as a dark room, or concealed warehouse, where they hope to hide their crimes, which, as fast as committed, are removed thither in expectation of never being found, or exposed to view, being secured by the lock of strong delusion under the care of carnal confidence, who carries the key of presumption, and is lord of all the lumber!

How very different are the declarations of God, who says, "The sacrifice of the wicked is abomination, *how much more*, when he bringeth it with a wicked mind?" Prov. xxi. 27. "He hath said in his heart, God hath forgotten; he hideth his face; he will never see it. Thou wilt not require it." See Psalm x. 11—15. "These things hast thou done, and I kept silence; thou thoughtest that I was altogether such a one as thyself; but I will reprove thee, and set them in order before thine eyes." Psalm l. 21. "Yea, also the heart of the sons of men is full of evil, and madness is in their heart, while they live, and after that they go to the dead."—"But know thou that for all these things God will bring thee into judgment."

To conclude,

It is hoped the above remarks may, through a Divine blessing, help entangled christians, respecting the following important particulars:

1. To behold and admire the equity of Jehovah's government, in requiring nothing above the capacity, or natural ability, of his creatures; and yet continuing the equitable demand of perfect obedience, and not altering his law in the least, to suit the base dispositions of his rebellious subjects; which would have destroyed every idea of authority, and sunk the reputation of God.

2. The necessity of the almighty operations of the Holy Spirit, in changing the bias and dispositions of men, by regenerating or creating them anew in Christ Jesus, and working in them to will and to do of his own good pleasure. For till the sinner's disposition be changed, till he be born again, and become a new creature, he can have no true love to God, no spiritual delight in his law, no approving views of Christ and his gospel. Yet the change produced does not destroy the natural freedom of the human will; but man acts differently from choice to what he did before.

3. By the distinction between natural and moral ability, sovereign grace is not only defensible

against every objection, but appears infinitely great and absolutely free. In every respect it is truly wonderful, because those who are saved were not only miserable, but inexcusably criminal, and as such under the sentence of eternal death, from which there could not have been the least hope of deliverance had not *grace* provided relief. If the several parts of the great salvation be surveyed, even from its rise to its final consummation, it will appear entirely of pure grace, infinite, unmerited compassion, and astonishing mercy, which could not be the case if moral death was not a blameable state.

Those who want to see the subject of grace treated in a masterly manner, and set in a clear convincing light, should peruse a book, entitled *The Reign of Grace*, by Rev. A. Booth, London.*

4. By observing this distinction, Scriptural exhortations to repentance and faith, appear quite consistent, which could never be defended if criminality arose from natural, and not moral inability.

In that case it would be equally as ridiculous to call sinners to repentance, as to exhort a blind man to repent of his continuance in darkness, and never behold the surrounding beauties of creation; and no less absurd than to attempt to convince the dead

* This excellent work is published by the American Baptist Publication Society.

of the crime of indolence, for lying in the grave. While sin is viewed as consisting in a natural defect, or a deficiency in the natural powers, penitence can never appear reasonable. For a man to pretend to repent, when at the same time he considers his fault to lie in a defect which he cannot possibly help if he would, is like a deaf man considering himself criminal because he did not hear to-day, and resolving not to be guilty of the like sin to-morrow. Indeed it seems to suppose, or require, a very great defect in a man's understanding, to be able to conclude, that such a repentance is what the Scripture recommends, and the godly possess.

5. The doctrine of natural and moral ability is calculated to afford much encouragement to seeking souls, and to comfort those who are really devoted to Christ. For as none *can* come unto him but such whom the Father draws, therefore spiritual desires after Jesus, and delight in religion, are *evidences* of a gracious change, holy dispensations, or a new heart.

You whose gifts are small, and natural powers weak, be not distressed, for grace is much superior to the best abilities. Therefore, rejoice, that the Lord hath shown you the more excellent way. Who hath despised the day of small things? The profane world and proud professors may; but God will not. Those who *love* the Saviour, to whom his person, blood, and obedience, are precious, and his ways pleasant, and whose desire is to walk humbly with God in the paths of purity, though they frequently stumble, and are discouraged, shall not utterly be cast down; (Ps. xxxvii. 24;) but shall hold on in their way, and grow stronger and stronger; Job xvii. 9. "They shall obtain joy and gladness, and sorrow and sighing shall flee away." Isa. xxxv. 8, 10. Those who are not able to plead on God's behalf, but love to think upon his name, are precious in his sight. They shall be mine, saith the Lord, in that day when I make up my jewels. Mal. iii. 16, 17.

6. The *strong* believer, however enriched with gifts and grace, should be led to various humbling and profitable considerations. However great his natural abilities are, he is as much under a perpetual necessity to look to, and rely upon the Lord, for gracious influences, as those of the weakest capacity; for a person may possess strong mental powers and be morally weak. Grace may be languid and low, where natural gifts are lively and strong.

While the christian is subject to sin, and a propensity to sin is felt, he will see the necessity of perpetual watchfulness, repentance, and prayer, and often cry, with holy Paul, *O wretched man that I am!* For though he is not under the sole dominion of sin, yet he feels and laments a criminal backwardness to good, and a proneness to evil. So that when he would do good, evil is present with him. He is the subject of two *opposite* dispositions, and therefore cannot do the things that he would. His resolutions are feeble, and his comforts fluctuate, because his affections are unstable, being sanctified but in part. Sometimes he mounts to heaven, and seems fixed on things above, but anon he drops down to earth and sense; and then he complains, and prays as David did, saying, "*My soul cleaveth to the dust, quicken thou me.*" He feels assured, that without Christ he can do nothing; yet he does not consider this as an *excuse* for the neglect of duty or the commission of sin. He does not bless himself that he has a bad heart, where he may safely deposit his iniquities, and thus keep his conscience calm.

But the sin of his heart is the sorrow of his soul, and his perpetual plague. It is the object of his hatred, and the subject of his secret and unfeigned lamentation: because he is taught to regard moral defects as inexcusable faults.

He longs for heaven, because it is a place of purity, where he shall be free from sin as well as from sorrow. While in the body, he considers himself neither where nor as he would be; therefore his desire is to depart and be with Christ, which is far better.

And as *he which testifieth these things* saith, *Surely I come quickly:* his heart replies, "AMEN, EVEN SO COME, LORD JESUS."

THE END.

INDEX.

THE END.

www.ingramcontent.com/pod-product-compliance
Lightning Source LLC
LaVergne TN
LVHW010253110826
845151LV00004B/1462